SERVANT LEADERSHIP

Sovereign Immunity Litigation

Coaching Your Inner Child

The Leadership I Ching

Leadership & Career in the 21st Century

Creative-C Learning

Integrate Your Emotions

Krishnamurti and the Psychological Revolution

The New Paradigm in Business, Leadership and Career

The New Paradigm in Consciousness and Spirituality

The New Paradigm in Science and Systems Theory

The Vibrant Nature of Life

Shamanic Wisdom Meets the Western Mind

Creative Genius

The Better Life

Servant Leadership

SERVANT LEADERSHIP

A Guide for Aspiring Young Leaders

by Peter Fritz Walter

Published by Sirius-C Media Galaxy LLC

113 Barksdale Professional Center, Newark, Delaware, USA

Set in Palatino

Designed by Peter Fritz Walter

ISBN 978-1-5088718-0-4

Publishing Categories
Business & Economics / Leadership

Publisher Contact Information
publisher@sirius-c-publishing.com
http://sirius-c-publishing.com

Author Contact Information
pfw@peterfritzwalter.com

About Dr. Peter Fritz Walter
http://peterfritzwalter.com

Pierre's Blog
https://medium.com/@pierrefwalter

About the Author

Parallel to an international law career in Germany, Switzerland and the United States, Dr. Peter Fritz Walter (Pierre) focused upon fine art, cookery, astrology, musical performance, social sciences and humanities.

From adolescence, Pierre wrote essays and received a high school award for creative writing and editorial work for the school magazine. Upon finalizing his international law doctorate, he privately studied psychology and psychoanalysis and started writing both fiction and nonfiction books.

In 1996, Pierre started his main career as a corporate trainer and personal coach. He trained the management staff of 5-star hotels in Java, Lombok, and Bali, Indonesia, as well as an elite unit of the Indonesian government (Lembaga Administrasi Negara), which trains all civil servants in Indonesia.

From 2000 to 2001, Pierre built a villa property in Seminyak, Bali (Dua Bunga) which he managed until he sold it in 2002. Likewise, from January 2011, Pierre managed two real estate companies in Pattaya, Thailand, until he sold his pool villas in 2014.

In 2015, Pierre extended his consulting business in the private sector, both online with self-improvement media content bundled in a subscription, and locally with presentations about the unlimited scope of our human potential, and the spiritual teaching of the late Dr. Joseph Murphy.

Pierre is a German-French bilingual native speaker and writes English as his 4th language after German, Latin and French. He also reads source literature for his research works in Spanish, Italian, Portuguese, and Dutch. In addition, Pierre has notions of Thai, Khmer, Chinese and Japanese.

All of Pierre's books are hand-crafted and self-published, designed by the author. Pierre publishes via his Delaware company, Sirius-C Media Galaxy LLC, and under the imprints of IPUBLICA and SCM (Sirius-C Media).

To Steve

The author's profits from this book are being donated to charity.

Contents

Preface

Why I Wrote this Book

This guide presents a novelty approach to understanding and training leadership for people involved in leading others not only in corporations, but also in the small and even the one-man business setting. For all leadership starts with effective self-leadership, the art to guiding oneself.

My approach is original in the sense that I brought into modern leadership training elements of ancient wisdom, thereby expanding the paradigm beyond the borders of the corporate culture. My approach also can meet the needs of an international lay audience that, today increasingly consisting of *free-lancers* from all around the world, is eager to build their leadership style, thereby raising their chances of a professional career beyond their national borders.

Let me expand a little on how I came to teaching leadership, for it's perhaps quite an uncanny story. When you look at my life before I turned toward the coaching profession, you will see so much misery that you will think I was really not born to become a leader!

To begin with, when I was in my teens I did not bother about leadership, but was sensitive enough to observe that both in my class in high school, and in the boarding, there were natural leaders, boys who were accepted by the others as leaders. They had some specific qualities that most of us were not endowed with, or not at that level of natural gift; and they proudly used these qualities and the skills that emanated from them to impose their ideas on us. They were often bullying us as well.

In hindsight I would say they had both positive and negative leader skills; hence, they were both positive and negative leaders.

Most of these boys actually abused of their leadership, which gave me to think early about what it means to be a leader. But after all, I did not ponder the question to the end, for otherwise I would probably have studied political science, and not law. To be true, I was rather putting a stress on their *negative* leader skills, which led me to reject the whole leadership question for many years.

This defensive reaction was not to my advantage; life got me to see where it leads to be so aloof regarding such an important question. I was always treated as negligible and others were leading the game, and those others were invariable stupider than I, lesser qualified, lesser sensitive, and had lesser wit. It paid in the wrong sense not to bother about leadership. To summarize, I was losing out on social success because of that very aloofness.

It was only in my forties when I started to think about leadership. In my fifties then, and not earlier, I started writing and teaching about it, and became aware that I had neglected a major topic in life, a topic that one should study and know about as early as in school. For fifty years, I had only randomly considered the fact that success in life almost invariably means to assume some or the other form of leadership, and that those boys in high school, or in the boarding, did that intuitively, spontaneously, because they had understood it, while I was struggling with my *negative connotation of power*, with the power that naturally goes along with leading others.

I was *connoting power with abuse*, and here my hangup came in, the rampant abuse that I had been suffering during my childhood and youth, and that I was projecting upon the words *power, leader, leadership, group, community*, and *society* as a whole.

When you do that, you are self-defeating. The truth is that when you assume expertise in any field of study, you automatically get on the leader track, if you are conscious of it or not. When you become an expert in any field of interest, you *become a leader*. It's as simple as that. That means we begin to exert some sort of social power or influence, as we are becoming 'an authority' in that particular field of study. Then, when that happens, and we refuse to assume that power, we may encounter reject and jealousy because others try to fill the vacuum.

When you are in a position of leadership because you are superior in one or the other way, and you do not assume the power of that leadership, you can be sure that others will try to take that power away from you. This is almost a universal law, and I have observed that mechanism over and over in my life.

And I have seen the negative side of this law in the lives of my parents. They had revolted against society, as they had to fight against Nazism in Germany when they were young; that they rejected all forms of power, including their own. This had very nasty consequences in their lives, as they were constantly envied by others and harmed through that envy they more or less unconsciously triggered in others. It was especially dramatic in the life of my mother who, after having studied and graduated in two majors, art history and journalism, was taking on, after the war, a simple government job. That was surely fine for a few years, as the country was steeped in poverty, but my mother felt there was a moment to step out, and she was dreaming to get the job that was her birthright, the post of director of our regional museum! The job was not available at the time, and my mother was patient, but her patience was eroded by negativism and the jealousy of her office colleagues who resented her being overqualified; on the other hand, my mother did not miss to let them know, and feel, that she was superior with her two PhDs in journalism and art history. And that marriage of contradictory behaviors was of course not a good one.

To make it worse, my mother was not promoted for several years and eventually sued the government via the trade union and won the process; but at that time her self-assuredness was so much eroded, and her mindset so bitter that she was giving up on the museum job. And it was right then, when the job became available!

I could talk and talk to her, encourage her to apply for the job, but she didn't. She let the opportunity pass with the argument that she had been waiting in the starting holes for so many years and was only a step away from her retirement, and that it was thus 'not worth the effort.'

What a big mistake! My mother had not assumed her power, she did not allow destiny to give her what she truly had deserved, worse, she resented destiny to have given it to her too late, and for too much of sacrifice. Unfortunately, in her biased perception of reality, my mother did not a moment think of the possibility that she may have delayed that turn of destiny through her constant negativism, and her bitter resentment. In fact, she had put aside opportunities to step out form the government and get a job in private industry or the radio. She actually had been proposed jobs in radio and television at several occasions, which was her expertise after all, but she refused them with the argument that 'these people are all perverse.' My mother regarded life, all in life, from a perspective of the past; she had been working at Berlin Radio during World War II and had made bad experiences with men who were members of the National-Socialistic Party. She hated them and the whole of the Nazi ideology. But this hatred was tearing her apart and prevented her from building inner coherence. In addition, she was virtually projecting the past upon the present. My mother thus never assumed a role of leadership in her life.

In that media archive, her government office, she had a sort of leadership, simply through her expertise, but she suffered from the jealousy of younger colleagues, who were backstabbing her. As a result, the director of that media library held by the *Ministry of Culture and Education*, where my mother was the only qualified librarian, was turned against her as a result of those intrigues.

This served me as an important lesson, as after my law graduation I had the opportunity to work for the *European Union* as a functionary in the administration of the *European Parliament* in Luxembourg. However, I did not accept that position as I knew from two German department directors who actually worked there that the work climate was strikingly similar to what my mother had experienced in her twenty-five years working for the government. I instead took on the very challenging task to do a doctorate in international law at the University of Geneva.

It was an exciting journey but a difficult one. I survived a suicide attempt and after that got all my forces together to finalize the doctorate which had been immensely difficult. Eventually, I got on a new track, after a psychother-apy and a prolonged sabbatical, and became a sales trainer and human resource expert, leadership consultant and coach.

It was a long journey, more than my parents had been through, more even than my grandparents had achieved; yet the essential was lacking: I did not assume the power that this profession gave me. I was still aloof to learn and assimilate what leadership is actually about.

It was only by becoming an expert trainer and corpo-rate consultant that I gradually became aware of what it takes to be considered a leader in one's field of expertise. Doing this work and helping others to improve their lives, their business and their relationships was, then, eventually the purpose I had been searching for in my life. My way to get there was not a straight line, but rather a spiral or what Thomas Moore calls 'the convoluted way of the soul.'

—Thomas More, Care of the Soul: A Guide for Cultivating Depth and Sacredness in Everyday Life, New York: Harper & Collins, 1994

The good thing about such a way is that once you ar-rive at your destination, you feel an immense burden lifted from your shoulders, and you see how useful and logical your convoluted path has been, and that you really needed all of the obstacles for experiencing growth and expansion. Then, your satisfaction may be material or it may not be material; you may earn little or much money in your new profession, but that, you will feel, is not the most important. The tremendous feeling of satisfaction you will then experience comes from the fact that your life turns out to be useful, that your work has a positive impact upon others and the world at large, and that you have found a niche where you belong, and where you can thrive!

Introduction

What is Servant Leadership?

This book is not about the old-style single leadership model that can be considered as outdated in the meantime. Since the 1970s we have a hybrid called 'servant leadership,' which sounds like an oxymoron, but is not.

The originator of the new leadership paradigm, Robert K. Greenleaf, wrote back in 1970: 'The great leader is seen as a servant first.'

In an essay he laid out the simple yet powerful concept which has become the *leading leadership model* now around the world. The oxymoronic nature of the term was purposeful and intended; while one may argue that not every leader is the opposite of a servant, this was at least so in our own occidental tradition. As for the teaching of the ancient Chinese sages, as for example Lao-tzu, they were very much in favor of a servant leadership paradigm while the technical term of course did not exist. Lao-tzu wrote in his Tao Te Ching:

> 17. High beings of deep universal virtue work unassertively. They help all people, yet people are barely aware of their existence.
>
> Leaders of great achievement earn the friendship and praise of people. Leaders of great strength make people afraid. People despise and defy a leader who is untrustworthy.
>
> One cannot inspire confidence in people through words alone; it must be accompanied by correct deeds. When one of subtle virtue has accomplished his task, all the people will say: 'It is we ourselves who made it so.'
>
> —Hua-Ching Ni, The Complete Works of Lao Tzu: Tao Teh Ching & Hua Hu Ching (1979/1995). Download my free edition of the Tao Te Ching in the translation by Peter A. Merel here: https://www.scribd.com/doc/209244479/Tao-Te-Ching

This is one of the best descriptions of servant leadership I have come across. Indeed, the servant leader is one who if ever possible will try to be nonobtrusive and lead through the example, instead of giving detailed instructions. He wishes his legacy to be one of the people having the last word, saying 'We did it all by ourselves.'

This is really the best and easiest way to understand the core meaning of servant leadership. So we realize that after all, it's not a new concept for there was at least one great sage in China who had precisely that vision 2600 years ago!

Now, back in the 1970s, Robert K. Greenleaf intentionally sought a descriptor that would give people pause for reflection, and challenge long-standing assumptions that were held about the relationship leader-followers in any organization. By combining two seemingly contradictory terms, negative historical connotations associated with the word 'servant,' he felt it a necessary choice to turn established conceptions about the organizational pyramid on their head, and jump-start into a new view of leadership. Behold, the meaning is 'The Servant as Leader,' not 'The Leader as Servant.' This is a subtle yet important difference for not confusing leadership with mere management!

In other words, as a *traditional leader,* you will tell people what to do from a position of authority but they will be much more receptive if you set a humble example yourself first. This is the way the *servant leader* operates because he or she knows that authority is something rather fragile, and if it has been used extensively, the leader is vulnerable to backlashes! If they feel that you can identify with them and you establish a common ground, they will be more receptive to follow your lead.

While there is no universal definition of leadership, there is agreement on the fact that leadership involves an influencing process between leaders and followers to ensure achievement of organizational goals.

According to Carol Smith, in her article submitted to *Management of Information Organizations*, Info 640, December 4, 2005, there are four tenets that present a fuller picture of the servant-leadership approach.

1. *Service to Others.* Servant-leadership begins when a leader assumes the position of servant in their interactions with followers. Authentic, legitimate leadership arises not from the exercise of power or self-interested actions, but from a fundamental desire to first help others.

2. *Redefining Relationships.* Servant leadership does challenge organizations to constantly rethink the relationships between people in the company, and even within nonprofits, and society as a whole. The theory promotes a view that individuals should be encouraged to be who they are, in their professional as well as personal lives. The more integrated validation of staff will ultimately benefit the entire organization.

3. *Sense of Community.* Servant leadership questions our ability to provide 'automatically' any kind of human services. Only groups consisting of individuals who are jointly liable for each other can perform this function. And it's only by establishing this sense of community among the staff that the organization can succeed in its objectives.

4. *Shared Decision-Making.* Effective servant leadership is best evidenced by the cultivation of servant leadership in others.

By nurturing participatory, empowering environments, and encouraging the talents of each employee, the servant leader creates a more effective, motivated work force and ultimately a more successful organization.

Now let us find out what the attributes of servant leadership are. Each of the above-listed tenets of servant leadership can derive only from the selfless motivation that resides within the leader. This foundation is distinctive to servant leadership and was not taken for granted in traditional single leadership, while it was *naturally possible* that even under the old paradigm, some leaders were doing their job in that manner, and most of the time very successfully so.

Servant leadership therefore emphasizes *certain core personal characteristics and beliefs* over any specific leadership techniques. Let me list here five of them, as adapted from Carol Smith's enlightening article:

1. *Listening.* The ability to listen is a critical communication tool, necessary for accurate communication and for actively demonstrating respect for others.

2. *Empathy.* Empathy is the ability to mentally project one's own consciousness into that of another individual. It is very important for effective leadership, and was so even under the traditional leadership paradigm.

3. *Persuasion.* The effective servant leader builds consensus groups through gentle persuasion; he does not exert group compliance through position power.

4. *Conceptualization.* The servant leader can conceive solutions to problems that do not currently exist. In this

sense, he practices *foresight*, a truly important ability for every leader.

5. *Stewardship*. As Peter Block shows in his book *Stewardship: Choosing Service Over Self Interest (1993)*, organizational stewards or 'trustees' are concerned with the overall good of the organization as a whole, and its impact on all of society.

6. *People Commitment*. A demonstrated appreciation of others, and an ongoing effort to encourage them and help them to grow.

7. *Community Building*. The rise of large institutions has eroded community, the social pact that unites individuals in society.

Mindful organizations can compensate a bit of this social vacuum by doing what society as a whole should do, namely, building communities that consist of empowered, and mindful, individuals.

Studies by behavior scientists confirm these characteristics as being critical to servant leadership (Joseph & Winston, 2005), while extending and clarifying this list to include many more leadership attributes (Russell & Stone, 2002).

So simplify, I will present here just two lists with those functional attributes, and accompanying attitudes:

Functional Attitudes

1. Vision
2. Honest

3. Integrity

4. Trust

5. Service

6. Modeling

7. Pioneering

8. Appreciation

9. Empowerment

Accompanying Attitudes

10. Communication

11. Credibility

12. Competence

13. Stewardship

14. Visibility

15. Influence

16. Persuasion

17. Listening

18. Encouragement

19. Teaching

20. Delegation

Now I will discuss the role of values in servant leadership. To begin with, I do not want to theorize that values are basic only to servant leadership; they are basic and were basic also for single leadership, which is why since quite a time we spoke about 'value based leadership' even before, or simultaneously to, the onset of servant leadership.

The above attributes describe the outward and manifest characteristics of a servant leader's behavior. One may argue that these attributes are natural as they grow out of the inner values and beliefs of individual leaders, and that personal values like fairness and integrity are independent variables that 'actuate servant leader behavior' (Russell, 2001).

This is by the way not something revolutionary and new, for as I pointed out already, in value based leadership, we are always defining values when we train leadership. I have done that always in my own approach to training leadership to the service industry in South-East Asia. But there are a few more values that are unique for servant leaders. (Russell, 2001).

This concerns primarily the servant leader's motivation, for the typical characteristic of the servant leader is that his motivation derives from a core, egalitarian belief which holds that those who follow are no worse than the one who leads.

Now, as to how values are communicated, it is known even from traditional leadership that values are not communicated by talking to the staff or making big promises; instead, leaders infuse their values throughout an organization through the process of demonstrated, observable actions.

While there are voices to be found in the literature among researchers that criticize servant leadership as 'unrealistic,' even to a point of saying that it 'ignores accountability' (Lee & Zemke, 1993), the overall literature on leadership suggest that the theory's emphasis on leadership motivation addresses the inherent weaknesses that reside in people. These weaknesses include a person's potential for error of judgment, as well as pride and self-interested actions, while servant leadership can and has overcome the typical 'subordinate relationships' that we know from traditional hierarchy based leadership. A leader who operates from a desire to first serve others avoids these power traps by building consensus, and empowerment of his or her followers.

In my experience with training management in South-East Asia over the last twenty years, there are important cross-cultural applications of servant leadership. When Robert Greenleaf introduced the concept of servant leadership back in 1977, his vision was that servant leaders are driven to serve first, rather than lead first, always striving to meet the highest priority needs of others.

Few people within the corporate world know that servant leadership has important spiritual implications and roots. I mentioned Lao-tzu already, but what even fewer people know is that the Bible reports striking examples of servant leadership, not only through the brilliant example set by Jesus Christ, as a spiritual leader. In her article in the *Journal of International Business and Cultural Studies*, Maureen Hannay from Troy University reminds us that Robert Greenleaf served 40 years as a business executive, which is why we can't dismiss servant leadership as a 'theoretical model.' Even more interestingly, Spears (Spears, 1996) has done biographical research revealing that Greenleaf was also influenced by a short novel, *Journey to the East*, by the German poet Hermann Hesse. He writes:

> '... Hesse's book is the story of a mythical journey by a group of people on a spiritual quest. The central figure of the story is Leo, who accompanies the party as their servant, and who sustains them with his caring spirit. All goes well with the journey until one day Leo disappears. The group quickly falls apart, and the journey is abandoned. They discover that they cannot make it without the servant, Leo. After many years of searching, the narrator of the story stumbles on Leo and is taken into the religious order that had sponsored the original journey. There, he discovers that Leo, whom he had first known as a servant, was in fact the head of the order, its guiding spirit, and a great and noble leader.' (Spears, 1996, 33).

Spears reports that Greenleaf concluded that the great leader is first experienced as a servant to others, and he believed that true leadership emerges from those whose primary motivation is a deep desire to help others.

One characteristic which continues to receive considerable attention in the leadership literature is empowerment. It has a central place in my own leadership seminars in South-East Asia.

The literature defines empowerment as 'granting individuals the permission to utilize their talents, skills, and resources, and experience to make decisions to complete their workloads in a timely manner.' (Gibson, Ivancevich, Donnelly and Konopaske, 2006, 500).

In many cases, this means that employees are making decisions about their work that were previously the domain of management. Managers must relinquish the traditional means of power and delegate some decision-making responsibilities to employees (Pollard, 1996). This involves entrusting workers with authority and responsibility (Costigan, Ilteer, & Berman, 1998). Empowerment is thus a key concept in servant leadership, and I have had that idea essentially *before* I ventured into the specialized literature, knowing it by intuition!

But perhaps my greatest contribution to servant leadership was that I discovered how badly a purely Western leadership paradigm performs in South-East Asia, especially a culture like Indonesia!

In the meantime, the insight has taken root especially in the United States that their national economy becomes more closely tied to the international economy; as a result, it is quite impossible to discuss management theory without some acknowledgement of the impact of cross-cultural contingencies. A management practice that works quite effectively in the United States might have disastrous results in Singapore, Malaysia, Indonesia, or Cambodia. This fact has been recognized regarding Japan even by major American corporations, but in a less insightful manner for other Asian nations. (This is due also to the fact that the Japanese have sought out active collaboration with American corporations for bringing about a mutually beneficial dialogue about leadership strategies, and the values that are at the basis of these strategies). Some researchers wonder if servant leadership is per se an 'international leadership model' but I think this assumption is quite daring and doesn't really provide practical solutions for our frequent cross-cultural dilemmas. It is smarter in my view to use a topological approach and coin a specific mix of leadership values for a specific culture, after having studied the inherent cultural values of that culture.

I have done that in Indonesia, for I started my research back in 1996 but only started my training seminars in 1998. These two years of research were well-spent. I used them to interview leaders in all the main sectors of the service industry, which are 5-star hotels, major banks, and travel agencies. Thus I booked appointments all over those years to talk to top leaders in the country who were in these industries, and got very valuable information about marketing strategies, performance problems, staff problems, and management problems. I made it a mission to study both local and foreign enterprises, in order to see if the problem was structural or if it was due to national educational values?

The result of my research was that the problems were not the result of national values, but had to do with the intrinsic disturbance of foreign investment in the local industries.

We know this problem from systems theory, while before the advent of systems theory, it was practically unknown.

Every interference in a system causes a *disturbance*. Systems are not only known from biology, the living systems we see under the microscope, living cells, and their organizational structure, zoology and finally the study of human society and living communities. In the teaching of systems theory, a systemic approach is one that takes into consideration that living systems are not organized in a hierarchy but though networks.

The evolutionary drive in this model is that networks can nest other networks so instead of a stiff rigid hierarchy, we get a structure that *nests networks within networks,* while all networks and sub-networks are instantly informed, and thus updated about the state of the system.

—Fritjof Capra & Pier Luigi Luisi, The Systems View of Life: A Unifying Vision (2014).

That means that if I as Corporation A will go to setup factories and do business in Country X, I will be going to disturb the business culture in that country, for it's a living system! Now, what can I do to not only successfully operate my business and thus make profits, but also get recognized as a company that benefits that country (which will ease my operations long-term as I will get goodwill from nonprofits and the government). The first and most important thing I can do is that I train my local staff not with a rigid leadership paradigm, and management strategy that originates form my own culture, but instead consult advisors who are teaching me the ABC of cross-cultural leadership, a variant of servant leadership that is adapted to that particular culture, while it *originates* from my own root culture (The United States, Europe, Australia, New Zealand, and so on).

So that means that instead of throwing my staff over the head with my own long-cherished training paradigm, I will look for a training approach that deeply, not only superficially, takes into account research conducted in that culture about how to effectively lead and motivate people.

Servant leadership fits this purpose ideally because it is not only free of the old ghosts of hierarchical superiority ('the next one in the corporate ladder will tell me what to do.'), but also of the newer ghosts of 'total performance ethics,' a paradigm coined in the United States, for Americans, which comes over in Asia and the Middle-East as a form of coercing staff into overdrive, thereby deteriorating their wellness and willingness to cooperate.

Needless to add that it's not a wistful leadership paradigm but rather destructive and short-sighted. Smart leaders will never even look at it.

Chapter One

Leadership and Management

Introduction

There is wide consensus that leadership is value-based. My own teaching of leadership is condensed in a practical and handy *6-Steps* scheme. While attitude training is important, it is unfortunately not enough for improving service commitment and anticipating customer needs. Hereafter I reference some useful books that I myself studied before I set out to formulate my approach to team leadership.

—See for example, Peter Block, Stewardship, Choosing Service Over Self-Interest, San Francisco: Berrett-Koehler, 1996, Edward de Bono, The Mechanism of Mind, New York: Penguin, 1969, Sur/Petition, London: HarperCollins, 1993, Serious Creativity, Using the Power of Lateral Thinking to Create New Ideas, London: HarperCollins, 1996, Stephen R. Covey, The Seven Habits of Highly Effective People: Powerful Lessons in Personal Change, New York: Free Press, 2004, 15th Anniversary Edition, first published in 1989, The 8th Habit: From Effectiveness to Greatness, London: Simon & Schuster, 2004, The 3rd Alternative: Solving Life's Most Difficult Problems, London: Simon & Schuster, 2012, and Karl Albrecht, The Only Thing That Matters, New York: Harper & Row, 1993

The businesses of both companies and self-employed people can only grow with the expansion of their customer base. This is why leadership training is on giving customer service the first priority. But what means *service excellence*, what means *supreme service?*

Let me say upfront that slogans cannot replace training and no quick and catchy formulas can replace the foundation of customer service attitude and motivation for the human capital of the company. I suggest to build the qualities needed within the *6-Steps* scheme that follows:

- ▸ **Step One**
  Vision Building

- ▸ **Step Two**
  Empowerment

- ▸ **Step Three**
  Servant Leadership

- ▸ **Step Four**
  Response-Ability

- ▸ **Step Five**
  Decide-Ability

- ▸ **Step Six**
  Create-Ability

Some of these concepts, such as servant leadership or *stewardship* are well established, others are my own creation. The corner stone among my proprietary concepts that I want to discuss here is *create-ability*. This term is combining the notion of creativity with another other term I've created: *decide-ability*.

Why do I not simply speak of *creativity?*

Edward de Bono has shown in his books and seminars that many of us have a problem with creativity. Obviously, artists, people who are creative on a daily basis, don't have a problem with it. Who has the problem, then? Those who are not creative, you may answer. Well, no. Because there are no people who are not creative. The people who have a problem with creativity are those who are creative as everybody else is creative, but who *think they're not creative.*

Creativity, in our culture, is usually taken for something extraordinary, reserved for select, highly gifted people called artists or geniuses.

By the same token, creativity is thought of as something vague and almost supernatural or, negatively, something wacky, crazy and off-the-wall. Most people in the corporate world, even in senior positions, do not take creativity serious. Or they belittle it and declare it was a mental concept. For example, Sergio Zyman, the famous marketing guru, wrote in his book *The End of Marketing (2000)*:

> Creativity is one of those magical, mystical words that marketing people throw around a lot when they want to avoid responsibility for producing results. But the truth is that creativity, like everything else in marketing, is not some unpredictable force of nature. It can be managed. You just have to understand what it is that you are doing and what it is that you are trying to accomplish when you are being creative.

—Sergio Zyman, The End of Marketing as We Know It, New York: HarperCollins, 2000, p. 168

What Zyman says is basically that creativity is just another element of management. His definition is a no-sense because it's no definition. He says that business executives should observe what they do when they are being creative.

The truth is that when you observe yourself when being creative, you kill every creativity in you. The observer is exactly the inner instance that has to be put to rest when we want to be creative; this is so because creativity is a form of spontaneity. Without being spontaneous, you cannot be creative.

What is the result of such a reductionist attitude? Lack of creativity leads to stagnation, to decay, to boredom, to a lack of new ideas. It leads straight to crisis. Where there is crisis, either on a personal, professional, community or even political level, you can be sure that before the crisis emerged, there was a lack of creativity and, as a result, of transformation and evolution.

The word *creativity* can be translated as *create-activity*, the activity to create. Creative action is one that is not just complacent, imitative or repetitive, but focused on finding new solutions to old problems. Anticipative action. That's all what create-activity is about.

Now, let us go a step further, and pass beyond create-activity, or mere functional thinking, and let us see what is *create-ability*—the power to bring about a new solution, to solve a problem in a new and constructive way, in a way that, for example, saves resources and is ecologically sustainable. Truly creative solutions often bear a quality of cost-saving or, more generally, an economic element in it. It means that they care for resources not to be wasted.

Create-ability, then, is the ability to find new solutions that are—

▸ Functional

▸ Problem-solving

▸ Integrated, and

▸   Original or unusual

Create-ability is the ability to step out of the common pathway and look around. But that's not all. It is more than that. It is one thing to perceive different solutions, and it is another thing to *do* those things, to implement the new solutions we've found. That is where create-ability comes in. It is a more encompassing concept than create-activity. It is based upon two qualities mentioned before, *response-ability* and *decide-ability*.

—The term 'response-ability' was coined by Dr. Stephen Covey, the author of many famous leadership books, among them 'The 7 Habits of Highly Effective People (1989/2004).'

When I am not *response-able*, it's because I'm so stuck in my usual pattern that I can't step out, broaden my mind, and respond to the novelty challenge. Then I lack responsibility and things may go wrong as a result. If I'm able to respond appropriately and creatively, I am *decide-able*.

After this overview of how we can build *create-ability*, I would like to discuss the implications of creating a service attitude which is customer-focused and that uses vision as well as vision-communication as its basic functionality.

The Six Jewels

The scheme that I mentioned indicates that we have to deal with six basic elements, that I call the '6 *Jewels of the Servant Leader'* or simply *'The Six Jewels.'* I will discuss each of these elements below and then summarize my conclusions. These six steps represent a kind of *road map* to our goal. But before I walk you through, we should have a look at the end result we want to achieve. What do we want to bring about when we look at leadership with the end in mind? Is it service? Or is it customer satisfaction? Or quality? Or a package of all of this?

I think it is tremendously important that we care about how to *define the end result* we want to achieve because how we envision the end result determines which way we'll take to achieve it. That sounds almost like quantum physics and in fact it has to do with it. If I envision a mediocre final result, is there a way to achieve the excellent package I would like to get? Obviously this is almost impossible.

Quantum physics confirms that we cannot look at nature without our conditioning getting in the way: we set up an experiment, and this very setup of the experiment in itself determines the outcome of the experiment, the scientific result. Or in the words of Fritjof Capra:

> My conscious decision about how to observe, say, an electron will determine the electron's properties to some extent. If I ask it a particle question, it will give me a particle answer; if I ask it a wave question, it will

give me a wave answer. The electron does not have ob-jective properties independent of my mind. In atomic physics the sharp Cartesian division between mind and matter, between the observer and the observed, can no longer be maintained. We can never speak about nature without, at the same time, speaking about ourselves.

—Fritjof Capra, The Turning Point: Science, Society And The Rising Culture, New York: Simon & Schuster, 1987, p. 77

Capra says that our vision of the experiment contrib-utes to how the electrons will behave. In more general terms, this means that our vision and inner setup, our very habit of looking at life determines the way life behaves to-ward us!

Thus, we co-create our world from inside-out, and it matters what's going on inside of us, what we set for being true, what we regard as our principles, our objectives, our vision, and our main goals in life! It is thus of decisive im-portance what I set out to be my standard.

Will it be a common standard, easily achieved by eve-rybody, or will it be a high, excellent standard that is hard or very hard to realize on a constant, consistent basis?

Once I set out to achieve a *standard of excellence,* does this not also influence the way I'm going to work for it? In other words, do you think it's possible to obtain an excel-lent outcome by using mediocre means? Don't the tools I use for achieving my goals need to meet the standard of excellence I set out for the end result? Obviously so.

I can perhaps afford to neglect one element, but I will certainly at a later stage be forced to remedy this lack of attention for detail. And as things are, it'll be more costly, more difficult, or more time-consuming to remedy the mistake.

To give an example. I am going to design a luxury four hundred fifty rooms hotel and forget to put hand sets in the bathrooms. After the grand opening, I suddenly realize that I forgot the wall phones and thus call the construction company. What are they going to tell me? They will say:

—Well, if you had said this right at the planning stage or even when we were in construction, we could have offered you a good price. It would not have been very expensive actually. But if you want to do it now, it'll be very costly. Can you imagine, we have to open the walls in each and every of the 450 bathrooms, get the connections, put the cables, fix the phones, close and paint the walls, clean up...'

I know a hotel where this happened. I was talking with the General Manager about the problem, but he shrugged his shoulders: 'Our budget would not allow it and therefore I do not even suggest it to the owners,' he replied.

Step One : Building Vision

It is tremendously important to *build our vision* before we even begin to plan. We do not design a strategy before we have cleared our vision because our vision *will determine the strategy we are going to take,* not the other way

45

around. In other words, we begin our journey with our right brain and not with our left brain.

A vision is built involving the right hemisphere of the brain, which has to do with associative, imaginative thinking, and not with logical deduction. If I remain left-brained and try to deduct logically, I remain in the past, because the premise I'm going to deduct from is within my existing pattern of experience. If I'm going to create something new, and this is what I want, I must step out of the existing pattern and *create a new pattern*. How can I create a new pattern? By envisioning the outcome.

Now you may argue that vision is much too general to be able to impact upon a strategy. Yes, a vision may be general at the beginning but it does not need to remain general. Visions can in fact be very detailed. The art is to derive the details from the general picture. It is like zooming into the picture, into the vision, to see the details. They are already there. I do not need to invent them. They are part of the holistic picture that I have got. Visions are holograms.

Vision building or vision clearing also involves to steer clear about what I do not want as a result; it may even be easier to begin with this *negative approach* first.

Let me again give an example from my corporate training practice. Back in 1998, I was invited to give a presentation to the government of a small country in South-East Asia. They wanted to modify their civil servants' vocational training, as they had a new vision of how a civil servant should act and behave in the future. It was quite an uncanny idea as they said they basically wanted civil servants having an attitude that focuses on the citizen 'as a customer of the government.' We brainstormed this idea and came to the result that we wanted to exclude from the start the traditional kind of civil servant. After the brainstorming session, we formulated our idea as follows:

'The traditional image of the civil servant was that they treat citizens as subordinates of the government. However, times have changed and we now want civil servants who regard citizens as customers of the government. Therefore, we want to exclude that old kind of civil servant right from the start.'

When you do that, you trigger a thinking process of how you can setup training to produce civil servants who are flexible, intelligent, well-informed, responsible, openminded and ready to take their job by the word, and so on.

And you bypass methods that you know would bring about the old type of stiff insensitive dread you want to get rid of. This makes you selective and determines the strategy you're going to take.

Step Two : Empowerment

The second step in *6 Steps* training is *empowerment*. Why do we need to empower humans to establish a supreme service structure in a company? Would it not be better to use obedient robots and let them carry out precise instructions?

Well, in a robot world where everything is predictable, this approach might possibly work. But we are not living in a robot world, we are fortunately living in a world with real and warm human beings, people who have emotions and who are at times irrational. What about your effectiveness in a scenario where you wish to give service to irrational beings by totally rational ones?

First of all, no human can be totally rational. Suppose it were possible to cut off somebody's emotions, that person would not be more integrated, but in the contrary more chaotic, troubled and less balanced. He or she will be little prepared to live in a human world with all the irrationality inherent in the humans of this world. So the person will be less adequate, clumsier, and have a lesser amount of emotional intelligence!

Have you ever looked around in excellent hotels and seen one or two of the waiters or clerks who are desperately clumsy? Have you noticed how maladapted, how off-track they seem despite their obvious motivation, and the excellent training they got and all the efforts they put in their work? You will see that the harder they try, the more effort they give to what they're doing, the more they'll be inhibited and the more they'll feel inadequate. What I want to say is that we simply cannot cut off the human element without getting undesirable results. The human element makes that despite all the training and experience we have had, we may feel inadequate, shy, poor. *We may lack basic self-esteem or self-confidence.* We may be withdrawn or aloof for one reason or another.

Empowerment means that persons are granted a space, an area in which they can achieve solutions in their own way, *safely.* The standards, of course, are given. This is true both for the director, and for the employee who cleans the floors. If the standard is *excellence,* the floor cleaning must meet the same excellence standard as the work of the direction team of the company.

Empowerment gives a space for decision-making, for new, alternative or uncommon solutions, and more than that, it gives a space for personal development. We grow through experience and first of all the experience to master a situation with our own resources, intelligence, and inventiveness. This space is the basis for our *response-ability.*

We are not responsible if we lack the space for making mistakes. When people are afraid to make mistakes they have never grasped what responsibility actually is about.

Thus they are basically unable to respond. They react but they can't respond. What happens when people are not empowered? They just obey; they follow, which means that they have stopped thinking.

And they also have stopped feeling responsible for what they do. Empowerment means to give people space to be creative with their own mind and to get rewarded for it at the end. Therefore we can say that there is a strong element of *motivation* in carrying responsibility.

Step Three : Servant Leadership

We are currently globally moving from a paradigm of single leadership to one of *stewardship*. There is a gradual, subtle change in how leaders perceive and define their role, their attitude and their basic vision about giving direction, motivating and managing.

Stewardship is by no means a new concept. Historically, the steward was the person in charge to carry out the tutelary role for a child-king. Stewardship was different from leadership in that the function of leading was associated with an additional function of *caretaking*.

You may take it lightly to do your job, but you may be more serious, more careful, when you do the same job for somebody else, especially when that person is a child.

Most people will actually be more caring in whatever they do when they do it for somebody else. Our *inner parent* will step in and act. The resulting satisfaction is one that comes less from our ego, and more from being concerned with the welfare of others. Welfare, as a value, is at the very center of stewardship.

It is not surprising that stewardship now emerges as a new paradigm at the highest level of corporate life! Too many concerns about environmental issues that are ultimately issues of human survival have given rise to public discussion and turmoil. Too many matters of ecological high-tech innovation have been disregarded or postponed over about the last two decades. Too many people have lost their jobs. Too many companies have quit the market and declared failure while the urgent matter of restructuring the economy remained untouched. All this happened in a climate where people were waiting for politicians to do something about it, but they remain waiting to this day, as politicians didn't for the most part do that important job.

Now we are perhaps one step ahead. We know that all of us are responsible for bringing about necessary change and reform, and that it's a mere excuse to wait for political leaders to do the first step. The politicians alone can't make it. The industry alone can't either.

This is so because the complexity and interconnectedness of ecological problems requires a new approach, one that is not linear and logical, but *nonlinear* and holistic. No single person or group can bring the solution, and no single nation; we are obliged to sit together and talk, to take a *systems perspective,* and become creative through exchange, interaction and intelligent cooperation.

Stewardship as a paradigm helps us to be more concerned about the periphery and the possible outreach of our political, corporate or private policies and the multitude of vibrations that every single action triggers.

Stewardship sees the caring aspect. It also facilitates the change from single leader decision-making to team decision-making at various levels of the corporation. More and more decisions, now and in the future, will be taken not by single individuals at the top of their organizations, but by top-teams, directional teams, and groups where all members are equally in charge for the wellbeing of the whole. Where there are more than one brain, the variety among human beings cares for brainstorming new solutions being more effective than a single leader brainstorming by himself or herself.

This makes that chances are higher that new and original approaches are found, approaches also that 'step over the line' of traditional or overly protective thinking. From there to create-ability is but a logical sequence.

Step Four : Response-Ability

Even under the antiquated single leadership paradigm, responsibility was considered an important and foremost value to be pursued in corporate culture. Corporate trainers such as Stephen R. Covey helped us to build awareness of the fact that response-ability is the very condition for quality service and, more than that, a fundamental attitude.

Covey teaches that there is *reaction* and there is *response*. Reaction is an immediate outburst of action that is not reflected upon. Response is the action that is aware of alternatives, that is mentally mirrored. In the ideal case response is caring, considerate and thoughtful, but not necessarily so. What distinguishes mere reaction from response is the use of our *inner space,* that is, awareness. Reaction is typically unaware of all the factors involved, including consequences. Response-ability, then, is the *ability to respond.*

Covey's way to re-spell the word rises our awareness to the point that we will easily associate some dynamic element in it.

Would you not associate *flexibility* with response-ability? Would you consider somebody being response-able who is deeply stuck in old habits, or else someone who is afraid of relating to others in a warm, personal, empathetic and caring way?

Actually, when you look around a bit, you notice that the value of *response-ability* appears to be declining among people in modern civilization. Despite this fact, for our achieving excellent customer service, we must deal with all the issues that are acting counter to easy response, such as anxiety, inhibitions, guilt feelings, lacking self-esteem, distorted self-image, and so forth. We cannot leave it to psychologists to deal with these important matters. We should put our trust in nature and empower our staff for being proactive about their problems, and thus help them initiate change from inside-out instead of waiting for sudden and often unwelcome change from outside-in.

Response-ability means also the inner strength to rejuvenate oneself through experience, to learn from past mistakes and to have a fresh innocent approach to every new challenge.

This is uncommon today, but very important. Success can be defined as *flexible adaptation to circumstances* while holding on to our inner vision.

Step Five : Decide-Ability

One step ahead and we are confronted with taking decisions. What about our *decide-ability?* It is not enough to be empowered, aware of inner space and able to respond. What are we going to do once we face different alternatives or various levels of priority?

Life often confronts us with decisions that we did not anticipate. Do we not need an ability to decide? What does that involve? The ability to decide simply involves *risk*, the risk to take the wrong decision, to make a mistake, to lose something valuable, to be erroneous in our assessment of the factors involved. If you never want to take a risk, you can never make a decision. You will be vague or fatalistic, and thus self-defeating.

Or else, you let others decide for you. Or life. That would mean you give up a part of response-ability by lacking decide-ability.

Step Six : Create-Ability

Create-ability is not just the end of our six-jewel lace. It is at the same time the beginning of it, in the sense that it will create a *new cycle*.

To check if you lack create-ability, you may find that you are time and again confronted with decisions that seem to fall upon you. If you cannot trigger change, you have to take a decision that *opens the flood gates* for change to come by its own volition. Or you may get to a point where you have to take decisions that force you to change your point of departure or your basic paradigm.

The company that refuses to innovate will face, sooner or later, a crisis situation and will have to take decisions to cut costs, unpopular decisions, decisions that nobody likes to take.

However, the cost-cut approach, as Edward de Bono showed in his books *Serious Creativity (1992/1996)* and *Sur/ Petition (1992/1993)*, is a weak and passive approach that comes into play only once growth was impossible or denied because of mental inertia, and lacking create-ability.

Cost-cutting as an approach to crisis is similar as modern medicine's approach to deal with disease. We cure the symptoms because we are afraid to know the true origins of the disease. It is *allopathic medicine,* not wise and preventive medicine. It is medicine that is unable to cure in the long run, by just alleviating a current pathological condition.

In human terms, the price of cost-cutting is high. There is hurt connected to it and often an unfortunate cutback in human resources. It is actually a high price to pay for economic health and further growth. It is the medicine that cures through costly and rather ineffective operations that cut the flesh away instead of healing it through the intelligent care of the moderate approach that practices anticipation.

Cost-cutting cannot remedy a lack of create-ability that was the trigger of the crisis. It is merely covering up the true source of evil. It is the preferred method of what de Bono called *the housekeeping type of management*. Truly, in crisis times the right thing to do is to invest more, not less, and become more active, not less, more creative, not less.

Time Management

We can easily observe that peak performance that is robbed from the body or the mind will severely damage the organism and, consequently, shorten life. Sport, as it is understood and widely practiced, is more of a sickening, than a healthy activity. It shortens life instead of prolonging it. Only because it is big business, it is so heavily promoted in the media, not because it is something valuable and worthwhile to engage in for humans.

Therefore, let's have a look at the opposite approach, which implies maximizing time while living with inner peace.

Thus our goals in peak-performance are these simple objectives, *maximizing time* and *creating inner peace.*

Peak performance in whatever field is founded upon maximizing time and living with inner peace. All the potential, all the output we need, be it as athletes or performing artists, be it as business people, is at our disposition once we can effectively maximize time and *at the same time* live with inner peace. When you closely observe success stories, outstanding and excellent achievements, you see that the persons who have accomplished those feats have the talent and the skills needed to maximize time and to live with inner peace.

Why do these two qualities help us achieve best performance? Because with more time we learn more and thus can realize more; and with inner peace, our inherent inner powers develop to peak levels because we are not trapped in inner conflict. Those who are at war with themselves cannot reach their highest potential in whatever field of life.

Let's have a look now at these two factors more in detail.

Maximize Time

All good people never have time!, I was told by a business friend some years ago. She herself, successfully managing a public relations firm, is one of them. Her agenda is always filled with appointments, but she manages to have a moment for a good friend, for a glass together, for her family and social obligations. Asking her for advice about finding a reliable secretary, she said: 'Take the one with the least available time, the one that is the most charged with work already!'

Her advice puzzled me at first. Wasn't it paradoxical? Would it not be wiser to take someone who is still vacant most of the time? Would such a person not give me more attention, and thus more of her energy for the work to be done? Sharing with my friend my doubts about her advice, she smiled and replied: 'No. You see, we are not today vacant and tomorrow busy. Human beings are either vacant or busy, during all of their lives, even as children already. There are the *vacant ones* and there are the *busy ones*. Haven't you observed that yet?'

I kept silent a moment and then nodded. 'So, have you already been as busy as you are now when you were a child?' I wondered. 'Of course!' she answered. 'And there were quite a few of those little girls, I remember, who were vacant. Nothing to do. Bored. And guess how they are today? They've nothing to do. They're bored.'

From this encounter I learnt one of the most important criteria to identify *effective people*. They all have one thing in common, they've filled agendas but they are able to manage time. And they can maximize time, the little time they've left, maximize it to such an extent that it sometimes seems a miracle. What is their secret? What is it that makes them so effective?

I did not find the answer in one day, although it is fairly simple: effective people *use their energy in a very economic way*. They do not waste energy, as most people do. They use their energy with conscious awareness because they are focused upon what they are doing. *They are focused generally.*

So let us ask, what does it mean to be focused?

It means to be aware of one's thought processes. Because thought is energy, thought consumes energy. The more we think the more energy we consume.

Thus, if you let yourself without controlling or channeling your thought processes, you are like a car parked with running motor, consuming gas without going anywhere. The more you indulge in thought, the less you can find inner peace, and the more you consume your life's *primordial energy,* the fuel for life you got from birth to make you live. Once you've consumed this gas, you will leave this body because your fuel is off for this life, and you will go on in another dimension.

Therefore, if you want to prolong this existence, you've to conserve your primordial energy, and limit your speech and thought because these activities, talking and thinking, consume much energy.

It seems that, until this day, with few exceptions, no educational system has ever taken into account the subtle rhythm and cycles of the organism.

No-Time Management

No-Time Management is a concept of mine which, it seems to me, is widely contradicted. And, by the way, it's not theory. Let me report the practice first because indeed, it was first. And the theory came later. In high school I used to write the best essays in our creative writing class.

The teacher would read them in front of the class, and the whole school knew me since there was general agreement that my creative writing abilities primed. Some of my texts were subsequently published in the school magazine of which I was myself a founder and editor.

But how did these essays come to existence? Well, in a rather unusual manner. I would sit one hour or more in my bench daydreaming, literally doing nothing. The others were already very busy writing or working out their initial sketches. For me there were no sketches, there was no time table, there was no plan. And then suddenly it came. What came? An inspiration, an inner feeling that I could begin.

And then I would just start writing, writing, writing, quicker and quicker, until my hand cramped and hurt, and until the ever last second of time allowance ran out. So it went on, writings, art, drawings, painting, music, piano or organ improvisations, scientific writings, too. All is born in that way, spontaneously and without any effort. And the theory is clear. Everybody can do miracles provided that they forget time and make peace, *peace of mind.*

What is peace? What are we talking about? Just sitting quiet? Sitting quiet may be one element of it, but not an essential one. Inner peace is a *special state of mind,* characterized by the two brain hemispheres functioning in sync. It means that mind and emotions are swinging in harmony. It's a condition where you leave the periphery of your being and move to the center. And this peace you feel then is the *self*—for the self is peace, and nothing but peace.

Most religions tried to teach people how to establish peace, and many moral theories have been invented and applied, all to no avail. Many religious people have flagellated themselves so as to eventually bring about inner peace. But peace that is forced upon is not peace, but inner turmoil, an emotional exhaustion.

At the outside there is continuous change, and change is the form of life that is appropriate in that realm. The state of affairs at the periphery is movement. The only way to establish true peace is to move away from the periphery toward the center of our being. *This is an inner movement.* And you don't need to travel around the world for finding a guru for that.

My contention is that the more time management you do, the more you get caught in the busy outside movements of life, the more you are dealing with the petty little things of daily life, the less you will bother with the fundamental issues of life—or of your business.

There is no essential difference in dealing with religious issues or business issues. The fundamental principles of life reign all matters, religion, business, marriage, education as well as eating, sleeping and breathing.

Some famous think tanks and coaches nowadays acknowledge that the daily schedule is a trap. They favor the *weekly schedule* that is a much more natural time span. This is certainly true, but let's go beyond and question the concept of time management as such. Or lets put it less aggressively and ask 'Can there be some sort of intuitive time management?'

It could be argued that deep down in us we've an inner clock. This clock regulates our biorhythms and thereby keeps us attuned to the challenges we face; it watches even the subtlest movement of time. If you question this, please consider how many times in your life, when you were just thinking of a person, this very person called you or ran into you—right at the same moment. And how many times it happened that you ran into somebody you just badly needed for a communication and could not find, for some reason or another? And how many times it happened that you made a new contact, for a new love or a new friendship or business relation, just because the other person was sitting next to you in the bus or the train, perhaps only for a minute, so that you could exchange your cards or phone numbers?

If this inner clock can time even the subtlest and most unpredictable events and synchronicities, it must be tremendously useful, and certainly should be relied upon, for *it knows much more than our rational mind can ever know*. It anticipates changes that so frequently throw rational planning into chaos.

Writing my little essays in school, I knew that I would block my creativity with plans and sketches. Nobody had told me. In the contrary. The repressive culture I grew up in taught me exactly the opposite. But I did not listen. I did not believe their credo. I knew better and trusted my intuition.

It seems to me that the almost hysterical *busy-ness* of today's modern world is not a modern phenomenon at all, but the consequence of an old premise. It is the *don't-use-your-intuition-but-stress-your-ratio* idea. This is truly a repressive concept since it represses life itself, its spontaneous and highly intelligent synchronistic expression. Life is nonlinear, not logical in the sense of mere causal connections. It contains a higher logic, a *logos* which is beyond the limited human intellect. It is so to speak synchronistically logical or holistically synchronistic.

Time and Peace

Nowadays more and more managers, and besides, other folks want to escape from this busyness in order to find the peace they need to listen to their inner mind, their subtle inner voices, their intuition. Many of them are conscious of the devastating effect a hyper-rational worldview had on their creativity. They want to rediscover the cyclic processes of life and, more generally, conceive the fruits of wisdom that life itself contains.

In the United States and Japan, among other industrialized nations, there is growing awareness about the need for this new form of learning not only within top management circles. America bears a precious treasure; it has the greatest teachers of humanity around: the native peoples. Two of them, Rainbow Hawk and Wind Eagle, a couple, the founders of the *Ehama Institute* in California, are now doing consulting with major companies such as General Motors and AT & T. What Rainbow Hawk and Wind Eagle teach are the fundamental, cyclical processes of living, processes that have their influence upon our daily business decisions.

They stress most of all the need of modern man to get connected again to our inner potential, to develop a regular habit to move back into our inner ocean of stillness and peace that is the self, and to base decisions upon a holistic view of events both from the perspective of our rational mind and from our deep-down wisdom or intuition. It is simply to overcome the deep schizoid split that repressive education has forced upon us.

It sounds a bit ridiculous that the guilt for this state of affairs is generally put upon a generalization called 'modern life.' It is in reality not modern life that creates the split, not the computer or the airplane technology and not the microwave or laser disc.

The culprit here is our human conditioning, a schizoid past and the fact we have never learnt, as a human race, what it means to live peacefully, namely by acknowledging and integrating our natural emotions. With peace it is a bit like with health. Peace is not all but without peace all is vain. Walking in circles like the proverbial tiger in a cage, we only create further problems, further stress and further confusion instead of resolving problems, reducing stress and getting clarity of mind.

Clarity of mind is not the fruit of intellectual training. It is the fruit of inner peace, for time and peace are interconnected and interdependent. In a way time is a function of peace. Where there is more peace, there is more time.

Knowing this, we can create more time in our lives by establishing more peace, by relaxing for example, by introspecting, by taking quiet intimate moments for ourselves at regular intervals, also by avoiding conflict through effective communication, and last not least by upholding the right attitude toward self and others, an attitude that is based upon openness, respect and truthfulness.

How much time do you spend on creating and maintaining, discussing and administrating conflict, problems and litigations, without ever penetrating into the true psychological roots of those conflicts within yourself?

In every conflict there is a periphery and a center. To solve a conflict effectively means to penetrate into its center, exactly as with resolving conflict within yourself. Thus, here we have a truth that applies both to resolving conflict inside and outside. But what is done instead? Conflicts are often shifted on other levels, renamed and thus *administered*—without being effectively solved; this means they are treated at their periphery only. Just as with modern medicine that treats the symptoms and not the causes, that cares about sickness but not about health, as it has, until this day, never defined *what health truly is.*

If we want to treat cancer and we destroy its symptoms by cutting out a tumor, but we do not look what really happens in the cell, in the essential elements of our organism, we cannot say that we really care about treating and healing cancer. And so the cancer will spread elsewhere in the body.

Peace Management

Once we see that time and peace are interdependent, there is only a little step to conceive the idea that in fact *time management is peace management.* To begin with, our language is incorrect for time itself can't be managed. Instead, affairs are managed in time and space.

Peace management is what Olympic athletes do. It is the management of peak performance. Sounds odd? Why? Because it sounds unusual?

Peace management means to manage affairs in time and space by managing them outside time and space. How can? To remain always within our time and space continuum means to exclude love and any form of higher wisdom, for all that is essential in life is not bound to time and space. When I say in other publications that my art is born in my creative continuum, I actually want to say that it is created outside the time-space continuum and born within the ocean of peace that we all bear in our inner self. The difference between me and you is simply that I recognize the existence of this *inner self* and that I deliberately developed ways to get connected to this inner treasure. I am not connected all the time, otherwise I would be a master or guru. But I am not a master and do not want to be a guru. I do not want you to be my disciple. I want to be with you on equal levels.

And from there we start in our work, not from a guru-disciple biased system. I am connected at times, or let's say more modestly, it lets me get into it at certain moments. *I can't say that I control the access.* I rather think that such control is an illusion because the inner self, or higher self is beyond control. In our work, then, what we can do, again modestly, is to facilitate the process in a way to prepare ourselves to be received by it.

This also implies to live with *purity*. I do not mean that by all means we need to be vegetarian or live an ascetic life. This may rather be counterproductive to peace if it is forced upon, if it does not come about spontaneously. Purity of mind primarily means to keep an innocent heart. It means to keep a healthy balance in all we do and also in all we think. Keeping a balance means avoiding extremes.

Peace settles on the way that is between extremes, as Buddha put it, calling it *the middle way.*

We know that many of us have a big problem with that, keeping a balance in all we do. Because it means not to judge, not to refuse, but subtly being conscious and, first of all, remaining sensitive to all. And flexible.

Our education, which is based upon punishment and reward, stresses the rights and wrongs, the white and the black, the good and the bad, the angels and the devils. It accepts partly and partly shuts out. It is literally the philosophy of half-heartedness. Its dualistic stress feels threatened to conceive the possibility of a tertium. The Aristotelian logic with its *tertium non datur* has profoundly affected our cultural tradition and makes for hassle, for quick judgments, for prejudice and yes, for violence.

If you expect me giving you a quick recipe for installing inner peace and creativity in you, I must disappoint you. I would be dishonest if I promised that. Because there is no quick fix to get out of all the quick fixes that an ignorant civilization made us buy into since the age of enlightenment which was actually the beginning of the age of darkness. But there is a way, a very personal one. But it is not a quick fix. It does not fix something since there is nothing broken that needs to be fixed. And it is in most cases not quick, but can take a lifetime or several lives.

But I recommend you to try this one, even if it takes you centuries. It is to *get in touch with yourself*—with your higher self. For once connected to your higher self, you will be guided on your own track and not any collective or alienating track you are on right now.

So every minute that you work on getting on this track is not wasted time, but the best investment you can do for your future. While it is a waste of a cosmos to stay one more minute on a track that is *not yours*.

The HeartMath® Research

The insights I formulated and presented in this chapter are based upon intuition and experience. I drafted them for the first time in the 1990s. I did not expect that one day scientific research would prove them to be true. But this has well been the case. Stephen Covey reports in his book *The 8th Habit (2004)* that controlled double-blind scientific laboratory studies 'are producing increasing evidence of the close relationship between body (physical), mind (thinking) and heart (feeling).'

—Stephen R. Covey, The 8th Habit: From Effectiveness to Greatness, London: Simon & Schuster, 2004, 51

Before I go more into detail using the original research report, let me outline here the quite far-reaching conclusions that Dr. Covey drew from it, calling it our four intelligences:

▸ Our physical intelligence (PQ);

▸ Our Mental Intelligence (IQ);

▸ Our Emotional Intelligence (EQ);

▸ Our Spiritual Intelligence (SQ).

The IQ is our classical intelligence concept as affirmed by psychology and early brain research. It was widened in the 1970s by the understanding of 'emotional intelligence' or EQ.

—See for example Daniel Goleman, Emotional Intelligence, New York, Bantam Books, 1995

Goleman writes in one of his later books, summarizing his many years of research on emotional intelligence that 'for star performance in all jobs, in every field, emotional competence is twice as important as purely cognitive abilities.'

—Daniel Goleman, Working with Emotional Intelligence, New York: Bantam Books, 1998, 31

The intelligence of our body, namely our gut, and our spiritual intelligence have however been discovered more recently only. Doc Childre and Bruce Cryer write in their research report:

> The human body is an incredible system—roughly 7 trillion cells with a mind-boggling level of physical and biochemical coordination necessary just to turn a page, cough, or drive a car. When you consider how little of it you have to think about, it becomes even more amazing. When was the last time you reminded your heart to beat, your lungs to expand and contract, or your digestive organs to secrete just the right chemicals at just the right time? These and a myriad of other processes are handled unconsciously for us every moment we live. Intelligence manages the whole system, much of it unconscious.
>
> The notion that intelligence is a purely cerebral, aloof activity uncontaminated and unaffected by emotions

has been shown in this and much other recent research to be an outdated and misguided myth.

—Doc Childre & Bruce Cryer, From Chaos to Coherence: The Power to Change Performance, Boulder Creek, CA: Planetary Publishing, 2004, 27-28, and 33

What I was trying to point out in my own words, that is, that *self-regulation* is built in our body and mind system, and that peak performance is a result of inner peace is now confirmed by HeartMath® research.

These scientists have termed the inner state that is conducive to success 'inner coherence.' Based on this insight, they are talking about the need for *inner leadership* and *internal self-management* as the starting point of all highly effective leadership. This revolutionary research confirmed what mystics already knew under the oldest of traditions, namely that the world is an 'internally created phenomenon.' We all live in a different world after all for we take the inputs received through our senses and process that sensory data through our mental setup, our beliefs and out emotions to create what each of us experiences as 'the world out there.' The authors write in their report:

Creativity, decision-making, health and well-being all improve when mind and emotions are coherent and relatively noise-free.

—Doc Childre & Bruce Cryer, From Chaos to Coherence: The Power to Change Performance, Boulder Creek, CA: Planetary Publishing, 2004, 3

From my several years of work experience as a corporate trainer in South-East Asia, I know that today organizations not just in Asia but everywhere in the world are challenged at a very high level. The mechanistic management solutions most executives have learnt and believed in are not working any more because they disregarded the human element, which means the human being that has also an irrational side, and is emotional, rather than an always rational robot. Under the old leadership paradigm and before globalization, this was still quite workable, but with the networked world economy and the relocation of producing markets to virtually everywhere on the globe, the old model proves to be increasingly in sufficient. It is not surprising, then, that the authors summarize their research in these alarming terms:

> In an age of chaos, emotional management or mismanagement is more important in determining the long-term success of an organization than product success or process improvements. This is as true of start-up firms that experience rapid success but are unprepared for its operational realities as it is for the massive older organization or institution affected by large-scale emotional turmoil and malaise of its workforce. It is also true that 80% of the Fortune 500 companies of 1970 have disappeared off the list.

—Doc Childre & Bruce Cryer, From Chaos to Coherence, 34

This is why the individual learning experience assumes such a great importance. When executives and workers in a company are left alone to self-manage their emotions and learn new knowledge, they will fall back on old memories, those namely they had in school or even earlier.

> Without conscious thought or choice, a person often avoids learning environments and challenges because of unpleasant feelings imbedded in neural tracks in our brains during earlier learning experiences.

—Doc Childre & Bruce Cryer, From Chaos to Coherence, 34-35

What this research also revealed is that the cognitive capacities of employees become far more sharp and effective as emotions become balanced, understood and integrated. If organizations continue to leave people alone and without professional support in handling their emotional conflicts and challenges, or believe that it's enough to have a psychologist in the house, they will not be able to help their staff handle the enormous stress that today is part of organizational life everywhere on the globe. Abundant research delivered the proof that millions of people today are maladapted to handle the stress of life in our modern consumer societies, both at work and at home.

—See, for example, Hans Selye, The Stress of Life, Revised Edition, New York: McGraw-Hill, 1978/1984, with many references

Hans Selye was the first researcher who found that not all forms of stress are harmful. He even asserted that some basic level of stress is needed for advancing in life; in other words, our emotional system can cope with stress if stress levels remain within reasonable boundaries. According to

HeartMath® research it depends on the person's ability to handle their individual 'stress response.' In so doing, a person skilled in self-management can actually take stress as an opportunity for personal growth. Thus chaos is not the problem; but how long we need to build inner coherence.

> Research in emotional intelligence has shown that the most successful people in life are the ones who have learned to manage their emotional reactiveness, neutralizing or transforming negative emotions in the process of gaining a new richness of experience.
>
> —Doc Childre & Bruce Cryer, From Chaos to Coherence, 43-44

This research also demonstrated that when the electrical patterns of the brain synchronize with the rhythmic patterns of the heart people operate with greater physiological coherence, resulting in increased conscious awareness and greater intelligence.

> The ability to self-generate feelings such as care, appreciation, and compassion is key to greater brain efficiency, enhanced learning, and a more emotionally balanced life. This is one reason why heart intelligence is such a powerful metaphor for increasing personal and organizational effectiveness.
>
> —Doc Childre & Bruce Cryer, From Chaos to Coherence, 45-46

One of the most cutting-edge findings of this research is that, contrary to more traditional neuroscience, people can learn to 'rewire' maladapted neural tracks that inhibit learning, growth, and emotional maturity that are necessary for achieving success. The brain has showed to have an enormous plasticity for those processes of rewiring neural networks and change preferred pathways that were laid down in early childhood.

This fact alone opens enormous possibilities for assisting employees with professional mind and brain changing tools targeting at not only boosting their performance level but changing their self-understanding in virtually limitless ways. We need, as a society, and even more so, as an employer, to stop blaming our emotional nature for mismanaged emotions and start to see the heart for what it is—the source of our core power intelligence.

This is so much the more important as, although the heart and brain each radiate electrical frequencies, the amplitude of the heart's signal is 40 to 60 times stronger than that of the brain!

A mind or organization without heart is scattered, impulsive, and easily distracted. Emotions and organizations without the intelligent balance that comes from the heart create flash fires of instability and waste, causing people to stay locked in self-justified mental loops, missing a heart intelligent perspective that could offer deeper understanding. Incoherences rules. People leave. Groups operating only on instinct arising from gut feelings and often based in fear stay constrained in modalities that imprison the spirit and age prematurely. The heart puts first things first, from the 7 trillion cells it nourishes to the life it sustains to the vitality it ensures—intuitive, intelligent, businesslike; core, fundamental; the first priority.

—Doc Childre & Bruce Cryer, From Chaos to Coherence, 51, 55

The results measured after implementing this research are staggering. They included reductions of 65% in tension, 87% in fatigue, 65% in anger, and 44% in intentions to leave the company.

The Mandarin Oriental Hotel in San Francisco was one of the first organizations that setup a program inspired by the HeartMath® research. But even before, the hotel won many awards for its consistency in providing exceptional value and service to its guests since opening in the late 1980s. Internal Quality Management (IQM), which is a self-management program was instituted at all level of the hotel staff to help ensure a high level of balance of personal and professional effectiveness.

The Zen Approach

Zen is an art of management, because it is the art of managing life. In Zen there are no theories. Yet it could be said that Zen is the purest form of management theory. Managing in the spirit of Zen means to be an *artist of life*, a human who is not ashamed of his or her humanness and who refuses to play the fake and fake the play many managers are caught in. It means to be *authentic* and without false toward superiors and inferiors alike.

Zen management means leading others by the strength of virtue, not by the power of command, while it does not for that matter follow a puritanical or a spartan life paradigm. Zen is not out to put restrictions, but instead focuses on maintaining a way between extremes.

Zen followers have less difficulties to be excellent leaders than those who are tough, demanding and try to be perfect. Nobody likes to follow a saint, because we know we are no saints.

Zen teaches *self-leadership*. The one who can lead himself can lead others. Self-leadership and self-discipline go hand in hand. However, the kind of self-discipline that Zen teaches is not rigid or moralistic. It is not judgmental but natural, spontaneous. To be *disciplined* is a necessity if one wants to follow the *Tao*. And it is a necessity for the manager. A leader who is disciplined but non-judgmental is followed with love; a leader who is undisciplined and non-judgmental is followed with half-heartedness; however the leader who is both undisciplined and judgmental is followed with hate.

Zen teaches wisdom and consideration by simply following nature. Nature is wistful and it cares about all beings without discrimination. The leader who follows the Zen teaching accepts his subordinates without discrimination; he cares for them as he cares for his own children. He does not judge them and does not offend them. This ensures him their devotion, also and particularly in times of crisis.

The Zen art of management is the *Zen art of life* because Zen and life are not different. The *art of life* and the *art of management* are two melodies played on the same instrument.

Practicing Zen means to be original, naturally oneself, and beyond circumstances, conditions, and environments.

Zen means leading by attentiveness, by awareness.

Awareness is twofold, inside and outside. To be aware means to be aware of one's own complexity, which is the infinite complexity of life. This awareness is virtue, and the secret of simplicity. Being aware of my own traps, I do not fall in the traps of the world.

The Zen leader may be alone, and he may be misunderstood at first. Others may wonder why he does not like to attend noisy meetings, why he does not overreact and listens carefully, and why he does not shout at his subordinates nor bow in front of his superiors. They may take him for an arrogant, picky kind of guy. But that is wrong.

The Zen manager is aware of what people are talking about him, but he does not interfere in their gossip. By no means does he try to justify himself, by no means would he explain why he does such and such. Does the sun justify why she is shining? Does the moon justify why she is only visible at night?

The Zen manager is confident that people *find out by themselves* what is true and what is false, and that this ensures their building trust in him.

The Zen manager, as all of us, has known many foolish managers but he does not force himself to be non-foolish. He knows that chasing the Buddha, he can never meet the Buddha. Thus, he can accept life, himself and others naturally, and without false.

Points to Ponder

▸ *Chapter One* was about defining servant leadership and internal self-management, with leadership as the overarching term. We have seen how we can achieve leadership by following a simple and comprehensive *6-Steps* scheme. It is a handy formula and guideline that serves as a roadmap for training to oneself and others effective team leadership in a time where the old paradigm of single leadership is not only frowned upon as outmoded, but also proves more and more dysfunctional in a network economy, and in the global setting.

▸ Last not least, it's not only a question of more or less of democracy at the top level of the corporation, but also a matter of check and balances. A team is naturally more apt to detect flaws in product design, marketing or promotion than a single leader, simply because 'four eyes see more than two.'

▸ The team leadership concept outlined in this book is a value-based leadership approach that works when values are consciously built and shared in a democratic manner, through incremental, strategic and systematic consensus building at all levels of the company. It consists of three basic constituent elements: *Servant Leadership Basics, Servant Leadership Excellence* and *Servant Leadership Values.*

▸ The *6-Steps* formula that I am using in this training guide consists of the following elements:

> ▸ Vision Building
>
> ▸ Empowerment
>
> ▸ Servant Leadership
>
> ▸ Response Ability
>
> ▸ Decide Ability
>
> ▸ Create Ability

▸ I explained why I am using the neologisms *decide-ability* and *create-ability*. When human creativity impacts upon decision-making, and the person has both the skills of *response-ability*

81

and *decide-ability,* regularly through solution-focus what results is *create-ability,* the ability to bring about original new solutions to old problems. New solutions can easily be recognized using the following criteria; they are typically *functional, problem-solving, integrated* and *original.*

► *Step One,* vision building, the starting point of our six jewels lace, is a moment of creative imagination, where our right brain is more active than our left brain hemisphere when we visualize the outcome. When we want to create novelty, we need to create a *new pattern,* which may require us to 'think different.'

► *Step Two,* empowerment, is necessary because only empowered executives can get into the positive spiral of *create-activity* by using their *decide-ability* in creative ways. Without empowerment, we would be stuck in fear and would feel guilty for every little space we claim for ad-hoc decision-making. In any kind of hierarchy, only explicit empowerment can create the necessary free space for employees.

► It is important to observe that mediocre organizations, those namely that lack vision and expansion power, are typically those that refuse to empower their executives. The result is that they can't work out a functional team leadership paradigm and have a 'boss' that reigns over the company like formerly princes ruled their kingdoms. Empowerment also implies to train executives in handling their *inner selves,* and their irrational side, to learn practicing self-acceptance, emotional coherence, and latitude of mind.

► *Step Three,* servant leadership, is the workable leadership paradigm for the 21st century, within our *globally networked consumer culture* that requires high effectiveness, flexibility and a response-ability for every corporation.

► *Step Four,* response-ability, is a skill that was even necessary under the old leadership paradigm. Response typically is different from *reaction* in that it requires an *inner space* from which to respond. When building a service attitude, we must deal with all the issues that are acting counter to easy response, such as anxiety, inhibitions, guilt feelings, lacking self-esteem, or a distorted self-image. We cannot leave it over to psychologists to deal with these important matters. We should trust nature and thus empower our staff being proactive about their problems, and thus help them initiate change from inside-out instead of waiting for sudden and often unwelcome change from outside-in.

- *Step Five*, decide-ability, is the ability to take ad-hoc decisions, especially in stressful and demanding situations, typically when a customer requires an immediate solution and higher-rank service officers are not available. In customer service, there is no time, so to speak, as customers have the right to get their problems solved in no-time. This is not a joke, but a goal, the goal of *excellence* in serving the customer. This standard can only be met with totally effective customer service reps who can make decisions on the spot, and have been thoroughly trained to do so without making major mistakes. Human perfection, while it's an ideal, as humans are by nature imperfect, is well possible to strive for. In the future, it's the companies who give the best service that will make it in the *totally networked international consumer culture,* not those who sell the best hardware.

- *Step Six*, create-ability is as it were the most precious of the six jewels, in that it's the *supreme skill* to develop through the training. An executive or civil servant who is create-able has the skill to make any decision needed in any possible situation ad-hoc, responsibly, and with a high level of accuracy and competence. It is also an executive who is in touch with his or her inner potential, the eternal present, thereby using *the power of intuition* alongside his rational problem-solving ability.

- As this chapter was also about self-management and managing affairs, usually called 'time management,' we were looking at different approaches for maximizing time by using proven principles applied in sports, and the training of peak-performance, as well as cutting-edge HeartMath® research. We have seen that without considering to imply our heart and conscience, and our inner powers, such as intuition and visualization, we would easily rob our body from resources if we applied a rigid scheme of maximizing performance.

Chapter Two

The Warrior of Peace

Why does our attitude have such a strong impact on performance? The answer is simple while the reality behind the answer is complex.

Attitudes are like glasses; they mold our perception, they define how we see the world, how we perceive reality.

This is why building an attitude is so important in self-development and in training excellence. In addition, our attitude has to do with relationships, the way we relate to ourselves and to others. And since relationship is an art, building attitude is an art.

Already two thousand five hundred years ago, *Sun-Tzu* (544-496 BC) developed a personal philosophy based on attitude rather than on belief or ideas. Sun-Tzu observed that the great general *Pan Lo* followed principles for mastering warfare what he called *The Art of War*. Sun-Tzu, inspired by Pan Lo's ideas, wrote a book with the same title, and this book, that was long overlooked, is today considered a foremost leadership manual.

—See Donald G. Krause, The Art of War for Executives, London: Nicholas Brealey Publishing, 1995

In fact, the principles Sun-Tzu discussed in his book have found to be universal; and quite surprisingly, they also have been seen to cover the *art of peace*, or the *art of relationship*. It can be said that business is an art, too, and this art is akin to the *art of relationship*, for business is relationship. When we are in business, we are in relationship.

When we work in a company, we are working 'in company.' Our language is aware of the intricate connections here between communication, relationship, and business!

To achieve a leader role without having the correct attitude is pretty much impossible! Leaders who boast with their smart and their achievements are respected, but seldom loved. Leaders who boast with anything are at risk in times of crisis, for they will be told to have not been smart enough to avoid the crisis in the first place.

This guide sets out attitude training in two major parts. In the first part we are going to extract some general principles found in Sun-Tzu's old *Art of War* teachings. In the second part we will see how to implement those principles by training them.

Sun-Tzu stated that the ideal general wins the war before the fight ever begins. He does this in two ways:

- By developing his character over time

- By creating a critical strategic advantage

Developing One's Character

Character is the foundation of leadership. It has to be developed over a long period of time. Character is the result of an attitude, built over time. Attitude can be defined as the way we relate to ourselves, to others, to the environment, to the world, and the universe as a whole.

The principles Sun-Tzu developed are still valid and valuable today, and they can serve us eminently for developing awareness what attitude is and how we can develop it. Furthermore, Sun-Tzu's book is an important source for teambuilding and leadership. There are principles Sun-Tzu applied for the successful organization and management of an army; these principles equally apply for the organization and the management of a business in the competitive environment of a market.

First Principle : Conflict Awareness

The first principle that Sun-Tzu taught, is *awareness of the roots of conflict*. He said that if we want peace, we have to be prepared for war. This means that the management of a company should always be prepared for competition. Note that, for example Bill Gates, in his remarks about successful management states unequivocally: *'Never underes-*

timate your competition!' Many of the principles that Gates applied and applies in his brilliantly successful leadership can be traced back to Sun-Tzu's teachings. I do not know if Gates has studied them; in fact it is not excluded that he did, which helped him later in the drafting of extraordinarily effective solutions for building highly productive teams within the large framework of *Microsoft® Corporation*.

This principle applies to working in a team. Peace and harmony and, as a result, productivity are best achieved if all team members are aware of the possible roots of conflict, first of all within themselves, and second in their relationships to the other members of the team.

Second Principle : Giving the Example

The second principle that Sun-Tzu taught for outstanding leadership is to *give the example*. This sounds quite familiar, yet it is often not observed. Not infrequently we expect from others what we ourselves are unable to commit to. If we require our staff to be honest toward each other, we have to give the example of honesty toward all of them, because others take us by our behavior much more than by our eloquence.

Third Principle: Sound Judgment

The third principle that we can draft after Sun-Tzu's writings is that leaders should be *well informed and realistic in their judgments and planning*. This means in practice to be prepared for the worst possible outcome, without however expecting it, and thus without being negative or pessimistic. This attitude has to do with *risk management,* with keeping risks as low as possible and as high as necessary.

Of course, there are always entrepreneurs who take great risks, engaging in large-scale speculation and making their fortune in a gambling-like manner. However, success brought about in this way is unstable and in most cases not a long-term affair, let alone a basis for future wealth.

Fourth Principle: Being innovative

The forth principle could be described as *being innovative* or at least open for innovation. Often the most expensive or complicated way of realizing things is not the most effective one. Great innovations always tend to be simple, and generally genius is regularly marked by an amazing and often surprising simplicity. In the run of affairs, it is easy to forget that every procedure and every habit can be changed, simplified and improved!

Being innovative simply means to be open for change and improvement and to consider *effectiveness as an outflow of simplicity.* Zen puts a strong emphasis upon simplicity in daily life and one of Zen's main virtues is to carry out simple and ordinary tasks as perfectly and as gracefully as possible. This principle, built into a large company, makes for effectiveness at a basic level. If all workers, from the car park guard to the president of the company carry out their duties with equal care, success is imprinted on the very fabric out of which entrepreneurial success is woven. The difficulty is to communicate to every single member of the company their value and the value of their contribution to the whole.

In Japan, *Shinto* accords the utmost value and importance to family bonds and responsibilities; because of this millenary philosophical tradition, professional teamwork in Japan is grounded in a fertile soil of spiritual roots.

There is mutual care from both the company toward the whole of its staff, and from every single staff member toward the company and its welfare. This is not just mere goodwill but a mutually caring relationship with manifold consequences and responsibilities.

Much of Japan's overwhelming success after its total defeat at the end of World War II was due to this spiritual traditional grounding of the professional work ethics. Furthermore, Japan has shown that being innovative at a large scale is not hindered by being traditional or even conservative. However, in Europe, where other values reign, conservatism has always been a major obstacle to innovation and beneficial change.

Fifth Principle: Professionalism and Excellent Communication

The fifth principle that we can derive from Sun-Tzu's teachings is a *high level of training and communication skills*.

We can even go as far as formulating this principle in our modern language in the way that success generally is a function of the human skill quality of the entire company staff and specifically of the management team. If the management team is ill-built and if communication is not flowing properly at the top level of the company, its chances for winning the market and even for mere market survival are poor.

Consulting experience steadily corroborates the truth that companies with a success attitude are always willing to invest in human skill training whereas companies that manage their market survival at the bottomline level cut or limit resources for staff quality improvement.

Supreme customer service, which can be seen as a common feature in companies that endure over long periods of time is a consequence not only of awareness about the necessity for customer care. More importantly, it is an involuntary projection of *the company's inner life,* the positive energy irradiating from the majority of happy and satisfied teams within the whale's intestines.

No trained-upon smile can make believe that behind the curtain everything is okay if it's not. Investing in customer care excellence is throwing money out of the window if at the gut-level of the company things are disorderly and chaotic.

We can thus summarize five principles derived from Sun-Tzu's ancient teachings as follows:

- Awareness of the roots of conflict;

- Giving and living the example;

- Being realistic yet positive;

- Being innovative;

> ▸ Caring for the best training possible.

Creating a Critical Strategic Advantage

The second point, according to Sun-Tzu's teaching of warfare, is to create a *critical strategic advantage*. We have seen that self-knowledge and the integration of our emotions are prime requirements for building character. However, building our character is not all. If we want to succeed, we also have to *act*. Acting in the market, in a competitive situation, means creating a *strategic advantage* for you, your product or your company. This is done by placing your organization in a position where it cannot be defeated while waiting for the competitor to give you an opportunity to win.

This means that you, as a person, and you, as a company, have to cultivate flexibility. What is flexibility? The market, as a natural self-regulatory system, requires from all its participants a constant effort of *adaptation*. We have to remodel ourselves and our companies constantly if we want to survive in a highly fluctuant environment such as today's and tomorrow's global market. In addition, there are certain character traits to develop which are necessary for succeeding. According to Sun-Tzu, these character features are:

> ▸ Being impeccable

> ▸ Being patient

> ▸ Being inscrutable

Being Impeccable

Being impeccable means to make no mistakes, to carry out one's business with the utmost perfection, expertise and experience. This may imply consulting experts instead of relying solely on one's gut feeling or intuition, or on folk wisdom. Being informed and keeping informed is essential for making appropriate decisions.

Being Patient

Being patient means to be able to wait for the appropriate moment to act. To make decisions is not all. They must be made at the right time. In the competitive situation, timing is crucial.

Patience is generally undervalued in the modern business culture. Being patient does not mean to be sluggish and passive. Patience is active watchfulness and readiness, and preparedness to strike at the appropriate moment. In this sense, patience is actually synonymous with persistence.

Life is efficient by being patient in often subtle ways. When you look at huge plants or trees, you may wonder how they could reach such amazing heights. In fact, when you contemplate them for a while you get the impression that they don't grow, simply because the growth of plants seems so slow to us. Yet they manage time effectively. The speed of their growth is controlled and always efficient. A huge banyan tree won't be surprised to find out one day, like some huge companies, that its growth was ill-timed and that it therefore has to shrink again in order to survive.

The wise leader is patient for she knows that ill-timed growth leads to non-growth or even to shrinking. Patience requires self-discipline and some kind of work on our emotions. *Growth is not linear, but circular or spiraled.* If you follow the line of a spiral with your eyes, you note that this movement implies also going backwards. And if you follow the spiraled movement for a short while, you get the impression that actually you always get back to the same point. It's as if you were standing still. All three movements of life are contained in the spiral that is winding up. *Evolution is spiraled, not linear.*

Similarly, positive growth of persons or organizations proceeds in a spiraled movement, not in a linear one.

Evolution and growth are always preceded by a phase of apparent stagnation or even a trend to go backwards.

Peaks are usually preceded by depressions, successes by breakdowns, major changes by hopeless inflexibility.

In the learning process the same scheme applies. Before we really learn something, we pass through a shorter or longer moment of doubt. When we grow inside, we stagnate outside. In the healing process, it is similar. Before healing takes place, there is a phase where illness seems to worsen. Strong bleeding often precedes real healing. The wise leader is aware of these threefold movements of life when she deals with her staff or subordinates. She knows that it is just in the moments when apparently there is no growth in people or progress at the outside level, or even a trend to go backwards, their inner growth advances.

The same applies to the life of an organization. Dysfunctional, ill growth occurs when one of the three movements was prevailing for too long. To repeat it, there is a time for going forward, a time for standing still and a time for going backward. *Success does not mean to go endlessly forward.* Success means first of all to have the knowledge when going forward is right, when standing still is appropriate and when going backwards is wise. In other words, success comes from the right movement at the right time.

Being Inscrutable

Being inscrutable means that wise leaders do not reveal their ultimate plans. At critical moments, spreading information can be defeating since the information can help the competition to take action and acquire certainty about strategic action keys, whereas without this information they would remain uncertain and therefore non-obtrusive.

The Warrior Attitude

The characteristics of enlightened leadership are in this present book described as the attitude of the *Warrior of Peace*. Let us have a look at this kind of attitude. It has two ingredients: 'Warrior' and 'Peace.'

What is a Warrior?

To begin with, what is a warrior? A warrior is someone who is on guard, someone who is attentive, who is watchful, who is prepared. A warrior tries to perceive as soon as possible the roots of conflict, for as long as the roots are small and young, they can be easily taken out. Once they have become a big tree, however, it will be difficult to get them out of the world again.

There are warriors of war and warriors of peace. The difference of the two comes from their inner mindset, their motivation, and intention.

The warrior of war fights for winning, the warrior of peace fights for harmony and understanding between all sentient beings. It is up to you if you want to be a warrior of war or a warrior of peace; the difference between the two is not that fundamental, by the way. It is less of a difference than between a warrior and a non-warrior. This is so because the gap is much wider between one who is attentive and one who is inattentive.

You may find it odd to associate peace with a war-like attitude, with preparedness or even with fighting. Yet the old Chinese sages said that if you want to have peace you should be prepared for war. What did they mean?

They meant that there are roots of conflict all the time, in ourselves and around us, and that we have to be watchful if peace is precious to us; watchful, namely, to perceive the tiny roots of conflict in every single moment, and prepared for fight, the fight namely to erase the roots of conflict as soon as possible.

The Warrior of Peace

The Warrior of Peace is thus someone who is *attentive* to the conditions that make for peace, which is more than just the absence of war. Where there is conflict, and as long as there is conflict, peace is impossible.

To bring about peace, we must *end conflict*. This is so inside and outside. Inside it is our conflicting wishes and desires that stand in the way to inner peace. Inner coherence cannot be forced upon us and we cannot really strive for it. What we can do, however, is to end conflict, erase the roots of conflict in us, and then inner peace comes by itself.

At the outside level, peace is only possible if we *end conflict with others*. However, in order to do that, we must first clean our own house and install peace inside of us. We do this by building awareness of the roots of conflict. What are those roots?

Well, thought goes in different directions. It is driven by contradictory impulses and emotions. Our emotions constantly change, like colors in a kaleidoscope; they recycle.

The Warrior of Peace Practices Acceptance

What can we handle our emotions so that they do not stand in the way to inner peace? One way would be to repress or to kill our emotional life. Many people choose this way, most of them unconsciously, by blindly adopting repressive educational and moral standards for their lives.

The result is that they split themselves off from life and agonize in uncreative emotional stuckness, unhappy and on the way to destroying their health and wellbeing. We are created as emotional beings, and emotions are highly important for our psychic and physical health, as well as for our creativity. Without emotions we are dead!

All the recent research on the roots of stress and functional diseases like cancer or immune deficiency syndrome has shown that at the basis of these diseases is an unhealthy and often punitive attitude of the patient regarding their emotional life. Such attitudes have their roots in our unconscious thought patterns and are regularly the result of social and religious conditioning.

Attitudes are the result of condensed thought forms; they make up inner programs that we carry from childhood. These inner scripts are sometimes a burden and an obstacle to success and wellbeing.

The way to go is first to *accept our emotions*, all of them, and give up judging them as being 'good' or 'bad.' Judging is something extremely counterproductive. Indulging in the habit of judging, we destroy creativity *because we destroy innocence.* Furthermore, judging deteriorates relationships, especially in the team.

In the work environment, there is often an attitude that boasts we were all 'rational beings,' and devoid of emotions. As if we could switch our emotions on and off. Such an attitude creates dishonesty among people. What usually happens is that in moments when we are inattentive, our emotions crawl into our team and seem to spoil every-thing. This is how we perceive it. Yet if things get out of hand, it is not because of our lack of control, but because of too much of control, namely because we want to control emotions instead of understanding them.

The Warrior of Peace Practices Permissiveness

The only effective control of emotions is *no control,* and *permissiveness.* Bioenergy research has revealed that wars are not the result of too much but of too little aggressive-ness; they are the result of our repressing natural aggres-siveness. This certainly sounds strange, yet it is the truth and has been corroborated not only by psychoanalysis. A simple example may show more clearly what I mean: if you let children play freely you can observe that they, too, have peace and war with each other. Yet when they fight, they never hurt each other badly until the point to kill or maim one another. The less repressive their education is and the freer they can express their emotions, the more balanced and the less destructive they are.

Destructiveness comes from repression, not from freedom. If you think that man is fundamentally bad because he's got emotions and is unable to handle them without a repres-sive system, you actually have no confidence in the intelli-gence that has created life in the first place. This intelli-gence has built strong survival factors in the essence of all living and would not create a being that is from its inner structure disharmonious and chaotic. If we feel torn up by our emotional needs or desires, or if we think that we can't handle some of our emotions, this is because we have repressed some of our inner energies, it is because the *emotional flow* is blocked somewhere in our organism.

Often this problem stems from restrictions or inhibitions imposed upon us in early childhood. If we get punished, as a child, every time we express a certain emotion we are likely to turn down if not completely kill this emotion off in us, simply because we need to survive!

And once we are grown up, we see that we are emotionally unbalanced, and as a result we need to do something about it, be it a therapy or anything that helps us to accept all of our emotions without judging!

The Warrior of Peace is Attentive to Emotional Flow

Repressing the emotion will lead to a discontinuous flow or blockage of the vital energy involved in the emotion. Whereas we may think that we control the specific undesired emotion or emotional response, we have in reality disintegrated this emotion and lost control over it. The emotion then has become problematic for us. When we feel that emotions get out of hand, we describe this fact with a language which reveals an underlying truth. We namely cannot handle what is out of the reach of our hands. In order to lead you back to a state of inner harmony, you have thus to *handle your emotions*.

One of many effective techniques for handling emotions is to engage in spontaneous art. Why can spontaneous art help you to integrate your emotions? The main reason why we have disintegrated our emotions is because we have divided them up in good and bad ones. *It is our judgment that actually blocks emotions.* In most cases the inner program that contains the negative judgment was written in our childhood days.

While in childhood we had no choice but to adapt to our early environment, however bad it was, as adults we have more autonomy and freedom in expressing our emotions.

However, our unconscious doesn't update itself automatically. The core of conditioning is thus carried forth beyond the circumstances in which it has been built. Pavlov's dog salivated when the bell rang, and not only when there was actual food for him, simply because the dog was conditioned to associating the ringing of the bell with the anticipated presence of food.

Likewise, people who have been traumatized in the war by bomb attacks, still crawl under the table when war is ended. Neurosis, as a pathology, is characterized by the carrying on of behavior which is anachronistic in the actual circumstances while it was appropriate within the original set and setting that brought it about. To get out of the spiral of conditioning is thus only possible if we can get out of the one who maintains the conditioning: the *thinker.*

It is our thought which is linked to the past, which is conditioned. However, there is a part in us which always remains innocent and untouched, and which is beyond thought. It is the mind behind the thinker. This part in us is not conditioned by thought as it runs not on thought, but on intuition.

The Warrior of Peace Values Spontaneity

This uncanny potential in us, which is our true intelligence, can be activated and strengthened by awakening creativity and spontaneity in our daily tasks and routines. In all we do spontaneously, there is no thinker and thus no judge. If you wonder what this potential may well be, you can recall a session of brainstorming in which you participated. Brainstorming is applied creativity and it is ideally an entirely spontaneous activity. Spontaneous art is manifold:

- ‣ Writing

- ‣ Visual art

- ‣ Sculpture

- ‣ Composing

- ‣ Dance

We can become spontaneous in a number of ways. Watch children or a genius like Picasso and you will notice that spontaneity is related to the very essence of life, and that it constantly refreshes and rejuvenates us.

Out of spontaneity grows creativity, not out of thought and planned activity. All art disciplines can actually be carried out in a spontaneous, nonlinear fashion. Spontaneous expression helps you to get out of purely linear thought processes so that your thought becomes more natural. All essential life functions have been coded in a nonlinear way, as cutting-edge systems research has shown.

The line does not exist in nature, as it is an intellectual construct, a mere concept, a direct result of left-brain thinking, while creative thought is nonlinear and can be compared with the form of the spiral which is itself a combination of two movements, the teleological movement of the line, and a second movement which is circular.

In the evolutionary spiral as we know it from natural science, there is a third movement which is something that leads upwards in a way, a movement that transports to a higher level. If the spiraled movement takes place on a two-dimensional plane, it would result in a filled circle. If it takes upwards to higher levels it becomes something like a staircase: think only of the double-helix structure of the DNA molecule, prototype of the code of evolution, written into life itself.

The Warrior of Peace is a Holistic Thinker

The difference between *linear thinking* and *holistic thinking* is essential. While the holistic thinker is able to apply linear thought where this is needed, the linear thinker cannot think holistically. This is so because the linear thinker engages only his left brain hemisphere whereas the holistic thinker uses the natural combination of left and right brain hemispheres. The difference, therefore, is brought about by the integration of the right brain in the thinking process.

Spontaneous art is a form of holistic thinking, and it intelligently uses our innate creativeness and becomes something like a motor of creativity. All of us are artists yet most of us do not know about their artistic potential. Art is not only the mastership of a certain technique or artistic ability, but a way of living, a way of being, of perceiving reality.

Spontaneous art is the ideal way to express and to integrate our emotions, and to bring our intellect in balance with our emotional life and our intuitive thinking. Besides, spontaneous art is *real art,* not just a therapeutic exercise!

Yet spontaneous art doesn't require a technique; spontaneous art work is typically accomplished in a few minutes, without any mental plan or sketch. Creating spontaneously, without worrying about ability or questions of technique means *connecting to our primordial pleasure to play,* the pleasure to create and to fiddle with forms, shapes and colors. In freely arranging them we can exteriorize emotions that are repressed and cause tension. The same is true for spontaneously composing music. The outcome of spontaneous artwork is that our thought processes will be more intelligent, and powerfully creative.

The Warrior of Peace Communicates Inside and Outside

Inner dialogue or *voice dialogue* is a cognitive technique that primes for getting in touch with inside, and for integrating all our different energies. For recovering and healing our *inner child*, inner dialogue is a powerful tool, as it harmonizes our inner energies and establishes a communication pathway within the psyche.

—See, for example, Hal and Sidra Stone, Embracing our Selves: The Voice Dialogue Manual, San Rafael, CA: New World Library, 1989

The most important aspect of voice dialogue is that it increases *self-knowledge*. Self-knowledge is the basis of the formation of attitude.

Without knowing who we are and why we are here, we cannot effectively work on building our character. This is so because we are all different and even principles that have proved to be valid for millions of other people may not be true for you, individually! Every principle, every teaching has to be tailored for us, and integrated into our own structure. This sounds quite uncommon and it is in fact disrespected all over the world, in almost all educational or vocational systems. We are still living in the era of mass-education with the inculcation of instant knowledge that is considered fit for every human brain.

One of the reasons why masses of people are uncreative passive consumers is the result of this uncreative educational system. Voice dialogue begins where school ends.

Self-knowledge, anciently taught as the ultimate path to God, is not very popular in our times, and it seldom is taught to children by parents and teachers because they themselves never learned to practice it and thus find it outlandish.

The Warrior of Peace Thinks Nonlinear and Holistic

Increasing creativity, working on our potential, getting onto the track of easy and highly effective achievement, to repeat it, is *not* a linear procedure. It is not like building a street.

Rather can it be compared to puzzling together a mosaic. Whereas in building a street there is a quite constant use of time, the time-bound work on the inner potential seems in the beginning very slow; yet as with doing a puzzle, to put the first stones is the most difficult. Once we identify the picture printed on the puzzle, we can finish it quickly. It is the same with puzzling out our *inner landscape*. Once we see the whole of it, once we make out the mountains, hills and valleys in us, we achieve our highest potential in a revolutionary short time. It can happen in one second! Yet it may take us years to make out the shape, size and color of the first stones in our inner puzzle.

The inner dialogue helps in identifying your inner picture, your inner landscape. When you go deep down in yourself, you may discover this space which is unpolluted and pure. In this space is hidden the true meaning of your life, and your original destiny.

It may not be accessible the first time you try to get into it. Yet after penetrating into our inner treasures, we can rescue them and realize our true ambitions.

The Warrior Virtues

Build and Train Your Inner Team

What is an inner team? Which persons in you form your team? Are they conflicting or harmonious in their interactions? How can you organize them so as to profit of their energies for your development? Identify your inner voices, personalize them, and build your inner team.

Once you master inner teamwork and all your inner team members cooperate, you will also be skillful in relating outwardly in a team setting and understand the power of teambuilding and creative teamwork.

Empower Your Inner Child

The child in us is the source of our creativity; it is the little genius in us, but also the little clown. It is always active when we are up to do something extravagant, something new, original and daring, or simply different.

The child in us carries us to new solutions, new horizons, new feelings and perceptions, and new experiences. Get connected to your inner child and find new and creative solutions to all your problems!

—See also Peter Fritz Walter, Coaching Your Inner Child (2014)

Easy and Effective Communication

We tend to project our inner mosaic onto the world, thereby creating our world according to our inner images, our inner landscape.

Communication with others can therefore only be as good as our inner communication is, the one we lead with ourselves.

Flexible Intelligence

The dinosaurs, as we learnt it in school, disappeared from the earth because they could not adapt to climatic changes. Similarly huge companies that were once blooming disappear from the market as their blown bureaucracies render restructuring and adaptation to the new market requirements impossible. Today more than ever before organizations should be watchful to not become dinosaurs. *Small is beautiful!*

Leading with Purpose

The *quality of customer service* is the outward reflection of a company's inner attitude. So it is with the teams that run the company. These teams should comply to the principles outlined above and their organization should be *purpose-driven and value-based*. Where their continuity is not absolutely necessary, they should be created ad hoc with a well-defined purpose, and dissolved once this purpose has been reached and fulfilled. Their term of existence should be defined from the very beginning. Their primary activity should be the effective gathering and processing of information. They should always be flexibly adapted to the needs of the company.

All members of a corporation's top team should keep in mind that teamwork is purposeful only if it serves the company and, in last resort, the customer. The human skill qualities, as part of a success attitude to be trained are the following:

▸ Be Peaceful

▸ Be Strong

▸ Be Flexible and Adapted

▸ Be Honest

▸ Be a Good Communicator

These qualities are especially important in team work. Let us have a short look at them:

Be Peaceful

What does it mean to be peaceful? Does it mean to sit at home the whole day and meditate? Does it mean to disengage completely? Does it mean to be passive and submissive?

No, peaceful does not mean to be passive or retreated, nor that the peaceful person has to be submissive, nor that she disengages from daily activities. Peaceful only means that inside this person there is peace. And as a result, what do you think will be around this person? Your inside attitude is always reflected outside of you, in your life, around you, in all your relationships.

Well, many of us know this and some may try hard to get there, yet with little or no result. Why is that so? The primary reason is that we can not chase after peace. Peace comes by itself. What we can do, I repeat it, is only to clean the floor, as it were, for peace to come, when we are ready for it.

We are not peaceful for very precise reasons. One falls into temper tantrums, another may try to master inner tensions by a stiff and inflexible attitude which drives others away and which we could identify as passively aggressive. What really does it mean to be peaceful? Does it not mean that we first are in peace with ourselves? Can we possibly be in peace with others if we are inside of us in a state of continuous war, strife and conflict? I think we agree on this point that outside peace means first of all *inner peace.*

But how to grow inner peace? That's one of the major questions humanity asked over the course of its entire history. We cannot just command us to be peaceful. We cannot force us to be in peace.

Peace seems to be the product of something totally different, a state where there is no conflict, or where conflict has ceased, and if it is for a moment only.

The way to get there? It seems that if we want to get out of conflict, we must first recognize that *we are in conflict.* This means that we cease to argue with ourselves, that we cease to deny the fact that we are conflictual beings. Let us get more deeply into this.

What is inner conflict? We have conflictual wishes and desires. Often our thought is contradictory or dialectic. We see the positive side of something, then the negative, then we try to make out a midway.

This is important for logic and reason and it is good as it is, yet it impedes us from being in peace with ourselves. At least for moments, we want to stop thought, we want to feel this immense inner space, this vast openness to infinity the sages of all times have experienced. We want to be like them. However, things are not that easy on the spiritual level. Wisdom is not something that falls from heaven like the Biblical manna; it is rather a gift acquired through self-knowledge, through a time-bound process of work on the inside level.

Be Strong

What does it mean to be strong? Do we have to practice *body-building* to be strong? I would rather suggest to do *mind-building* since our mind controls our body and not the other way around. What we do in attitude training is in fact mind-building; it is work that makes us strong inside.

If we want to find out what it means to be strong, we should first inquire what it means to be *weak*. It may be easier to find out its negative reflection.

Well, inner weakness is an attitude that allows outside forces to hurdle us around, pretty much in the condition of a vessel caught in a storm. A warrior certainly is someone who is in control of his movements, of his decisions, of his life. He is not much affected by outside forces; his actions are determined by his inner strength, his convictions, his principles, and his virtues.

It would be wrong to say that he is completely unaffected by those forces. Whereas someone is weak who is totally dependent on others. Somebody who is strong has gained some sort of mastership in handling relationships. It's the primary task for the Warrior of Peace to master.

Take the example of a small child. A baby is dependent on his or her mother. We call that *symbiosis* or fusion. There is an umbilical cord linking the two during gestation. Even after this physical bond is cut, a psychic umbilical cord remains which links mother and child for the first eighteen months of the newborn.

This example is not far-fetched. Often between adults, too, we can identify emotional or affective bonds which may have the quality of a pseudo-symbiosis, until a level which is pathological.

We can therefore conclude that a weak person is one who relates to others via codependence whereas a strong person relates to others on a basis of mutual freedom and interdependence.

Be Flexible and Adapted

Why do we need to be flexible? The reason is simple. If we are rigid, we cannot adapt to life and its movement.

Life is not stiff, but constantly changing. When we are flexible, we follow the subtle changes of life and change as well. When we are able to change, we are like the serpent. We leave behind our old skins and can adapt easily to new life situations and challenges. A large part of our hurts and problems come from our inability to change and our being stuck with the past and past experiences.

If we want to change, we have to *discharge the burden of the past* once in a while or, better, every day.

Meditation is a powerful means to let go and to get rid of thought and emotions that belong to the past and that have no more relevance for our actual life. Flexibility is a form of intelligence.

Be Honest

Successful communication is based on truth. Honesty is a major facilitator of human interaction. Truthfulness is a character trait to be found in successful people. It is truly a component of leadership. Building truthfulness has to do with reducing fear and building high self-esteem.

The higher the fear potential, the lower the chance that the person dares to say the truth. Truth needs courage.

Be a Good Communicator

What is the major obstacle to easy bonding and communicating? Of course, it is fear! Fear is a major obstacle in every process of communication; it makes that we hide things; it distorts communication at its very root. Fear can be reduced by reducing stress, as well as by integrating our emotions by means of spontaneous art.

Master Fear

In any form of initiation fear is involved. Fear is a psychological barrier, a kind of *inner doorkeeper* protecting the sacred new fields we want to explore. Fear is what makes us human. All great myths tell us that even gods are not free of it. Thus, fear is natural.

But besides natural fear, which is the fear of some real danger, there is *psychological fear,* as Krishnamurti called it, which is actually a form of general anxiety. The late psychotherapist Alexander Lowen called it 'fear of life.'

—J. Krishnamurti, On Fear, San Francisco: Harper & Row, 1995, and Alexander Lowen, Fear of Life, New York: Bioenergetic Press, 2003

Warriors transform fear into courage. The 11th Arcana of the *Tarot de Marseille*, entitled *The Force*, tells us about it.

This arcana can be associated with Hercules who conquered the lion by integrating its force. Hercules achieved victory over the lion in the sense that the lion became his secret and invisible-invincible agent and associate, his power animal.

Handle Emotions

If we follow Hercules, we integrate our emotions by first recognizing them as our invisible agents and associates. We do not judge nor repress them. We master them in the sense that, recognizing their existence and necessity, we *integrate the energies contained in them* by removing all obstacles to the free flow of those energies. All problems that we possibly have with our emotions come from the fact that emotional flow is inhibited or misdirected. That's why *passive attention* of our emotional flow, also called 'emotional awareness' is of such high importance if we want to integrate our emotions.

Develop Courage

Fear and courage are related since they represent the same energy. Courage is sublimated fear. The hero was at first a coward like Socrates who deserted from the army yet drunk quietly the deadly potion after he was sentenced to death. When we deny fear, we cannot develop courage.

Cope with Stress

Stress relief? Unfortunately, today many training approaches for coping with fear do the contrary: they provide distraction from fear by raising fear.

Jumping from a bridge as it is now offered in corporate training programs does not prove, in my opinion, that one has courage, but only that one is caught in the web of fear.

Jumping from a bridge is not mastering fear, put putting fear in prison, until it breaks out again. In addition, coping with stress, as fear is a form of stress, by enhancing stress looks a bit like treating alcohol addiction with drinking even more alcohol. It should not be overlooked that the body has limits.

If we want to master fear only with our mind, while mistreating our body, the body will take revenge and mistreat us accordingly. We'll get sick.

Therefore I propose dealing with fear by relaxation and by practicing positive acceptance, thereby facilitating inner coherence.

Have you ever observed that when you stay a moment with your fear and really focus upon it, and do nothing to escape from it, your fear vanishes?

Yet for many of us it is extremely difficult to really accept fear or, more generally put, things that we consider negative in us.

However, the only way to master the negative is to accept it and to abandon all the subtle techniques of the mind to escape from it.

Accept Yourself

J. Krishnamurti has given us supreme teaching of this truth, not only on a theoretical basis, but with a very practical and straightforward attitude. If you want to follow this teaching, you need to accept yourself at a very deep level. It is this acceptance that makes for change and that will be at the basis of true success. Self-development stops then and gives way to self-acceptance which truly is the highest form of self-improvement.

Points to Ponder

▸   *Chapter Two* dealt with the *Warrior of Peace* leadership training approach.

▸   When we ask what a 'warrior' is and we see that the prototypes of warriors are to be found in native cultures, and learn that the foremost quality of a warrior is *attention*, we can only wonder how such a quality can be built in a society that preaches distraction and entertainment almost like a religion?

▸ Yet we have seen in this chapter that while being a marginal exemplar in the set and setting of the modern corporate world, the *Warrior of Peace* makes for effectiveness, and can become a model servant leader, if only the top range of corporate leaders set their mind to it.

▸ This being said, there are manifest reasons why the *Warrior of Peace* is a superior business and government executive, to a point to be superior to all the models that preceded him or her. First, it's because this person is value driven. Second, it's because that person is acting in accordance with universal laws, by being peaceful. Third, it's because that person is highly attentive, not a moonwalker and daydreamer who 'sits through his hours' in the office, because he is connected with his inner realm of existence, his soul level, and his inner selves. Forth, it's because that person gives the example, has a sound judgment and is innovative in their basic character and orientation in life. And fifth, because that person is an excellent communicator.

▸ We have seen that, in addition, *conflict awareness* is one of the foremost warrior qualities, even and especially in times of peace and prosperity. When a company grows fastest it is most vulnerable to being attacked, to being outcompeted, or to being sidetracked into dangerous waters. Conflict awareness is something that was not part of attitude training under the old paradigm, where a business executive had to be 'nice and smart' first of all, 'smiling' and 'decent.' Under the new paradigm, these qualities while they are still desirable, have second priority after *attention, commitment, accountability, response, decide and create-ability, and a sound sense of premonition* that comes from a sharpened intuitive mind.

Chapter Three

Team Interaction and Direction

From Dependence to Interdependence

What is relationship other than projecting our inner dialogue upon the world, and into our relationships? The inner dialogue is prior to dialogue with others.

Without having built your inner team and unable to communicate properly with your various inner selves, you are not going to be a good communicator. Next, you need to build your relations with others, for good communication can logically only take place in good relationships.

Here are the three steps in personal evolution you will have to take to get there:

▸ Grow from dependence to interdependence;

▸ Leverage positive attitude and win-win;

▸ Relate emotionally to others without becoming entangled.

Here we deal with the delicate topic of dissolving dependency patterns and develop true and lasting interdependence with others. This transition, if it ever takes place, is for many people a matter of constant hurt and strife, and therefore assumes particular importance in every single process of personal achievement. To relate in a sane manner to others, you must have built a sufficient amount of autonomy and thus of independence. This is so because as long as you are fusioned with others, you lack the inner space to acknowledge the individuality of the other, their difference!

The topic of dependence, independence and interdependence is often overlooked in teambuilding seminars, and it's admittedly a tricky matter. My insights on the subject which grew during many years of personal and scientific work are presently shared by a growing number of mental health and coaching professionals.

But initially it was an avant-garde position in the years during which I found the solutions to my own emotional problems through the methods I developed and that now are the core of my human skill training. Just about a decade and a half ago these topics were the exclusive domain of psychiatrists and psychologists.

Stephen R. Covey, in his book *The 7 Habits of Highly Successful People* is very outspoken and clear about it. He states that success in relationships is impossible if we cannot make it *from dependence to interdependence*.

—Stephen R. Covey, The 7 Habits of Highly Effective People: Powerful Lessons in Personal Change, New York: Free Press, 2004, 15th Anniversary Edition, first published in 1989

It is interesting that Covey does not say we just have to develop independence, but well *interdependence*. However, independence is the necessary transition between dependence and interdependence. Let's make the point what the precise steps to be taken are:

Dependence

Fusioned with others

Independence

Disconnected from others

Interdependence

In flexible exchange with others

Fusion is extreme dependency. There are forms of living which require it, not only the plant realm. The human infant is indeed so dependent on the parents, especially the mother, that we talk about postnatal symbiosis for the first eighteen months of the infant. However, if things develop normally, this fusion or symbiosis should gradually take an end and develop into independence and autonomy.

When this happens, later the adult will usually develop natural synergy with others, and build the ever most creative form of relationship there is, *interdependence.* Unfortunately, many of us got stuck in this process of growing into real communicators, most often because the *primary fusion with the mother* was inhibited in some way or was emotionally charged with negative feelings. The result is that we carry into adulthood sequels of our primary fusion. This means that there is in us a secret need for dissolving our ego in the fusion with a loved partner, a guru, or a sect. We try to get very close to others to a point that the borders between the you and the me dissolve, or, if this is not possible, we tend to reject the other and feel abandoned or rejected ourselves.

Harmonious relationships are impossible when one or both partners of the relationship are stuck in dependency.

This is valid for the private sphere, and especially marriage, but also for business relations and relationships with employers, employees and colleagues.

However, you can change the pattern if you want to, by simply analyzing what gets you into power-struggles with others? Power-struggles are futile discussions, one-to-one or group interactions where you or the other person more or less consciously try to win the other over for your point of view, while each of you are focused only on increasing their own power at the detriment of the other's power.

This is something so deadly common in our times that most of us are more or less unaware of the destructiveness of it all. We often feel exhausted or insecure after such kind of interactions. We may also feel anxious and uneasy. Either we feel we've been hurt or we feel uneasy because we have hurt another and want to apologize. What is the missing piece in these relationships? It is freedom.

Power struggles inhibit personal growth. They often cause relationships to stagnate or break off. They destroy trust. They affect negatively our emotions. They trigger psychosomatic illness such as ulcer, cancer or deep depressions, and this both in our personal and our professional relationships.

Awareness of the problem leads, if we are responsible at all, to immediate and total action. This action consists in the following:

- Avoid power struggles at any price;

- Play the superior part in offering support for understanding;

- Develop pro-activity to build trust and security around you;

- Help the other overcome negative emotions.

Our ability to respond to others largely depends on our level of personal evolution, and our freedom from getting stuck in power struggles. The more we are dependent, the more easily we *re-act*. The more we are autonomous and interdependent, the more we *pro-act*. Pro-acting means that we have some kind of inner space for reaction. This space gets larger and larger the more we have developed creative acting in relationships.

Human beings display various responses to events or circumstances and tend to behave in unpredictable ways under emotional stress. However, we do possess that inner freedom to respond with conscious awareness instead of being driven by emotions reactions.

As humans, we do not follow instinct like an animal. Although we are conditioned socially and culturally, we've got the conscious power to change this conditioning so that it's more in harmony with the universal laws which are also the laws of success.

The necessity to avoid power struggles is vital. Relationships in which there is power struggle can't develop into a level of high synergy where the energies of all partners merge into an x-times higher form of power which will produce new and astonishing results. It is absolutely essential if we want to develop effective teams that we have dealt creatively with the issue of power struggles. In my work with groups I have seen that power struggles are the one and major point why teams fail, why groups cannot develop *createamity*, or creative team activity. If there is only one person in the team who is out to control the others, the whole group will suffer from it.

Once the group has identified the delicate control issues, it will react proactively to the one disturber and give him or her the chance for *positive evolution* helping to identify that person's control problem. Naturally, if the person does not want to change over a set period of time, the team will dismiss the person because of the destructive impulses that risk to endanger the synergy of the group as a whole.

Being proactive means to play a somewhat superior role on the stage of personal interaction. It means to offer support through empathic communication, understanding and clarity on words. This does not mean to always play the ambassador. At times it is more appropriate to just clarify things and take the masks off.

Unveiling the disturber should be done in a manner that is *respectful* toward the person's vulnerability and self-esteem. Having someone losing face is not appropriate to help that person develop their communication or relationship skills. All depends on the way we handle the problem in the team. In relationships we should observe the rules of tact and the social conventions.

To be honest and clear does not mean to act counter to those conventions, or to be tactless.

When we empathically relate to others, from our heart level and not only from our intellect, we establish a certain level of mutual safety in the relationship that creates the pathway to tackle even the most delicate issues.

If this safety valve, which could be called a *minimum standard of trust* has not been built, it's not possible to deal with such issues without endangering the relationship as a whole.

Helping others to solve dependency issues is not easy. It requires that we previously have dealt with these problems ourselves, and thereby identified our hangups and perhaps found creative solutions to them.

To facilitate change in others requires us to have done some personal work ourselves.

Team Interaction and Direction

Teambuilding is vital for survival, yet an art that can be learned. Why is teamwork important? Teamwork is but a form of relationship.

Today more then ever before tasks are divided in different specialized areas and competencies. Those different areas, for example departments in a company, must interact with each other to fulfill the requirements of the whole unit, the company. As a result of this situation, teambuilding abilities are increasingly important. It can even be said that they are vital for any kind of company in our times and that every success of the company as a whole is catalyzed by the successful action and interaction of the company's top management team.

Relationship is based on communication. Communication is the beginning of all relationship. To build our relational abilities, we need to nurture and finetune our communication skills. It is especially the silent or hidden part of communication that contains a dialogue about the values that we need for building lasting relationships. These values are first of all *trust, commitment* and *honesty.*

We normally do not talk about those things. We do not reveal our perceptions if or not the other person makes a trustworthy impression on us and if or not we are willing to invest in the relationship with him or her. Yet, without talking about these things, we communicate about them!

We do this in a silent, smooth and nonverbal way, using body language and a a whole arsenal of other signals.

We also use alibi-language to receive a more reliable form of feedback regarding these communication elements which actually build the relationship.

In the usual communication process, we do not get a feedback, or at least not a direct feedback, about our way to communicate. It means that much of the results of our communications remains hidden to us. There are especially two gray areas in every communication; it is how the receiver perceives us as a person, and how well the receiver understood the message we communicated

How can we get feedback if we use body language correctly and at our benefit?

We need a *teamwork facilitator* who observes us tightly and reveals us where our weak points are; with that kind of feedback, we can begin to build powerful communication. In addition, cultural differences play an often unpredictable role in screwed-up communication and make for a number of misunderstandings.

Behold, communication is not always rational! Those who know about and accept their own irrationality can control it and avoid confusing messages. One who wants to lead others must be connected to his non-rational potential, the inherent source of creativity and success.

Let us take a closer look at *synergy*. Building synergy is often crucial for building and maintaining teams. We can also talk about *team synergy* as the motor for building any kind of group or team. It's something that glues people to each other in a non-harmful way, in a way that is positive, stimulating and good for growth and evolution. The 'glue' is nothing other than *our heart energies that are melting in a positive way,* thereby creating more energy, or a surplus of energy, and it is this *surplus of energy* that later materializes as success and financial profit.

What is Synergy?

Stephen R. Covey is to my knowledge the first human skill facilitator who really stressed synergy as something vital and often crucial for the success of a people, organizations, and even nations in their relations to one another.

—Stephen R. Covey, The 7 Habits of Highly Successful People, Powerful Lessons in Personal Change, New York: Free Press, 2004, 15th Anniversary Edition, First Published in 1989, The 8th Habit: From Effectiveness to Greatness, London: Simon & Schuster, 2004, The 3rd Alternative: Solving Life's Most Difficult Problems, London: Simon & Schuster, 2012

Of course, the principle of synergy is not new; it is a very commonly experienced fact of life.

As often is the case, the things that we consider natural are generally not reflected upon. We don't really wonder why we experience a great evening in the opera or why we had a successful house party; we do not make fuss about a friendly talk with friends when having a glass together; neither do we write articles about a job meeting that really was a nice moment to pass since all participants seemed to respond easily and voluntarily to each other. And yet, all these experiences are moments of synergy!

What then is synergy?

As I have pointed out earlier, synergy is *a melting of vital energies,* something that comes about rather spontaneously but which can be prepared by working on our relationship skills and by doing our inner work first. Synergy is sometimes expressed with a mathematical formula like *One plus one equals three.* This formula expresses the fact that the result of a synergistically created product is more than its parts.

There are lots of examples for this fact in the world. A large and successful company like Microsoft® Corporation could not have been built if Bill Gates did not have the idea and conviction that personal computers needed software, and did not choose the right people, the most gifted, talented, intelligent and hard-working people to help him build his empire.

And he comforted his people, he chose them very carefully and once he had hired them, he offered them superior work conditions and first of all, a warm and creative work atmosphere in small and later on in large teams.

What is Createamity?

The idea of creative team creativity or *createamity* is one of my creations. *Creative Team Activity* is possible in teams that function on the basis of synergy.

There are many teams around, that are not synergistic. Why? I think it's worthwhile to really find out about this. The answer to this question will perhaps provide us with the key to the know-how for creating synergistic teams. I have put it in the formula: 'Deal creatively with problems instead of creating problems from problems.' In the synergistically functioning team every team member gets easily feedback from others about—

—Their self-vision;

—Their vision of others;

—The accuracy of their visions.

Such feedback can help tremendously to gradually build the vision that is profound, sound and far-reaching.

Once we find out that our way of doing was wrong, we can analyze why this was so. The team will help us to get the necessary feedback. Our way of doing can have been wrong for various reasons, to be discussed further down. Generally, team feedback will enable us to establish new ways of doing things, both individually and in the group.

You may argue that as all this is also possible individually, it should be the same in the team. Why should a team function differently from an individual human?

Well, in a team the situation is of course more complex than in an individual relationship because feedback can potentially occur far more often, regularly on a daily basis.

This is a good thing to happen for this constant feed-back looping in the process of teamwork makes that people without much effort improve themselves constantly.

There is another powerful motor for team synergy, it is *solution focus*. Solution focus really is a key to team success!

There is no better way to channel the team's positive energy and to enhance that energy than to build team focus.

Directing the attention of several people on *one and only one* task delivers powerful new results.

Every leader knows this secret! And yet it's easier said than done. If one has already difficulties with oneself to get focused on a task or a goal in life, how does one want to get to focus others' attention to it?

It means that the team leader must have the basic skill to focus his energies on single tasks and to carry them out successfully. He must have team qualities within himself. He namely might use the inner dialogue to build and train teambuilding skills within himself, by training it onto his inner selves. We do this in building and training our inner team.

How can we organize our interactions in order to profit of their energies for the development of our team? The answer is that we identify our inner voices, personalize them and build our inner team.

Once we master inner teamwork and all our inner team members cooperate with us for the solution of one common task, we will also be more skillful in relating outwardly in a team and understand the power of teambuilding and creative teamwork. In this process, our *inner child* is the most important inner entity, simply because this inner child is among our inner entities the most repressed one, the one we disintegrate most as a society.

Become a Team Interactor

Let me propose to you now a quiz destined to boost your awareness of the requirements that come with working in a team. I facilitate the task a little giving you a multiple choice of situations that may or may not be detrimental for the integrity of the team. Just underline the answer you choose or make a circle around it. Further down, you will go through another, similar quiz in your role as a team director. This will render you aware of the fact that these two roles are quite different, while there are well overlapping zones.

The answers are given at the end of the chapter. Please check them out after completing the test.

> *The team leader organizes the team in a way that there is harsh competition between the team members.*
> Detrimental // Not Detrimental

> *One team member secretly plays the spy for the boss.*
> Detrimental // Not Detrimental

The team meets only once per week for a discussion group.
Detrimental // Not Detrimental

The team is suddenly enlarged by new staff.
Detrimental // Not Detrimental

The team members ignore the names of their colleagues' spouses and children.
Detrimental // Not Detrimental

The team interacts only via company email. Besides that, the direction does not like people talking to each other at the work place.
Detrimental // Not Detrimental

The team meets twice per week in the gym and once a week for volleyball.
Detrimental // Not Detrimental

The team leader suddenly changed. The new team leader does not know the names of all the team members.
Detrimental // Not Detrimental

There is one person in the team who always contradicts.
Detrimental // Not Detrimental

The team suddenly blocks in discussions or meetings with other teams.
Detrimental // Not Detrimental

When the team members were asked to admit a new team member to a shared social activity, they refused because the new one came from a culture they disliked.
Detrimental / / Not Detrimental

The team members don't say 'Good Bye' to each other when they leave the company in the evening.
Detrimental / / Not Detrimental

The CEO of the company is a good friend of one of the team members.
Detrimental / / Not Detrimental

The team leader is authoritarian. He wants the team members to carefully listen to him and then carry out his orders without contradiction.
Detrimental / / Not Detrimental

One of the team members is a genius. He often comes up with ideas that question the traditional way of doing things.
Detrimental / / Not Detrimental

From Small to Large Teams

It's a well-known fact that teams experience difficulties to pass from small scale to large scale.

We've already shortly discussed the problem of enlarging the team and found that it is not per se endangering the team. However, in practice there are many factors involved that can undermine the team's *basic synergy.*

In larger teams there are *more built-in stress factors* than in small teams. The danger is a general loss in communication or communication becomes superficial to a point that basic emotional values are no more communicated.

This means *empathetic communication* will get lost and with it one of the strongest building stones of synergy.

There are not many companies who have mastered the delicate transition from small and highly effective teams to larger and very large, yet still effective teams as well and as creatively as *Microsoft® Corporation.*

Michael A. Cusumano and Richard W. Selby relate in their book *Microsoft Secrets (1995)* that Microsoft is a young company in the sense that it has achieved to uphold a basically new and modern paradigm which is *making large teams work like small teams.*

—Michael A. Cusumano and Richard W. Selby, Microsoft Secrets, How the World's Most Powerful Software Company Creates Technology, Shapes Markets and Manages People, New York: Free Press, 1998, p. 409.

The authors enumerate *six vital points* responsible for Microsoft's success in making large teams work like small teams:

1. Project size and scope limits

2. Divisible product architectures

3. Small-team structure and management

4. A few rigid rules to force coordination and synchronization

5. Good communications within/across functions and teams

6. Product-process flexibility to accommodate the unknown

Envision Yourself

Here we will look at the typical role situation in a team. We will focus on the question: *How can I as a team member contribute to the team developing more synergy, more creativity and more productivity?*

Would you like to give your feedback on that question? If yes, please write in this box what comes spontaneously to mind.

How I envision myself being a team interactor

Jot it down in a few seconds ...

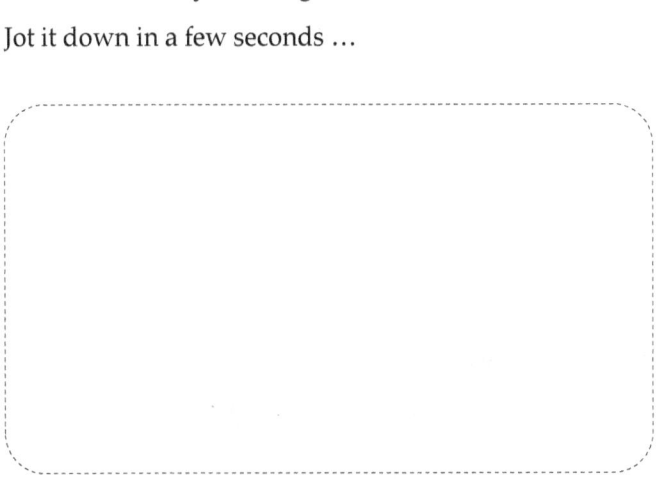

What do you think are the qualities needed or the values in play if somebody is effective as a team interactor, which means being an actor who acts proactively and interactively in a team. I mean a person who is procreative in the team in facilitating the team's developing more synergy, more positive communication, and more results.

Please try out this little multiple choice test to develop your own answer to the question of team creativeness and its facilitation through the team members' values and focus. Underline or circle around where you agree with the answer. The right answers are to be found at the end of this chapter; check them out after completing the test.

I would try every occasion to sabotage the team
Appropriate // Not Appropriate

I would be solution-focused and get the team solution-focused.
Appropriate // Not Appropriate

I would incite the team to review former decisions.
Appropriate // Not Appropriate

I would just tell everybody around about the team's qualities.
Appropriate // Not Appropriate

I would use diplomacy and tact to get the members involved.
Appropriate // Not Appropriate

I would play the contradictor.
Appropriate // Not Appropriate

I would invite the team to my house for a TV evening.
Appropriate // Not Appropriate

I would play the nice guy and shut my mouth.
Appropriate // Not Appropriate

I would play the team's Socrates and ask them silly questions.
Appropriate // Not Appropriate

I would talk first to the team leader to get my voice heard.
Appropriate // Not Appropriate

I would listen to all the team members and try to understand.
Appropriate // Not Appropriate

I would put posters on the walls that say 'Build synergy!'
Appropriate // Not Appropriate

I would not care because that's the task of the team leader.
Appropriate // Not Appropriate

I would first talk with my lawyer in order to know what to do.
Appropriate // Not Appropriate

I would do nothing. Because I have my work to do.
Appropriate // Not Appropriate

Become a Team Director

Here we deal with the role that the team leader should play to help the team develop *synergy and effectiveness as well as solution-focus*.

If you like to begin this section with giving your opinion on the role of the team leader or director, write in this box what comes spontaneously to your mind.

The best way of doing this is to simply imagine yourself being a team leader and then say what it feels like and what you would do in this role.

How I envision myself being a team interactor

Jot it down in a few seconds ...

What do you think are the *qualities needed or the values in play* when somebody is effective being a team director, the leader of a team? I mean a person who is proactive in facilitating the team developing more synergy, more positive communication, and producing more results.

Please try this little multiple choice test to develop your own answer to the question of *createamity* and its facilitation through the team director's values and focus.

Underline or encircle every question which answer you think is appropriate:

> *I would tell every team interactor what he's to do and what not.*
> Appropriate / / Not Appropriate

> *I would be solution-focused and try to get the team solution-focused.*
> Appropriate / / Not Appropriate

> *I would responsiblize the team for all its previous decisions.*
> Appropriate / / Not Appropriate

> *I would hang around the localities and invite people to small talk.*
> Appropriate / / Not Appropriate

> *I would use diplomacy and tact to define creative tasks for everybody.*
> Appropriate / / Not Appropriate

> *I would simply show them that I'm the boss.*
> Appropriate / / Not Appropriate

> *I would invite the team to my children's birthday party.*
> Appropriate / / Not Appropriate

I would play the ignorant and shut my ears and eyes.
Appropriate / / Not Appropriate

I would give the team strict guidelines and fire people if necessary.
Appropriate / / Not Appropriate

I would talk first to the company director to ask him what to do.
Appropriate / / Not Appropriate

I would first listen to all the team members and try to understand.
Appropriate / / Not Appropriate

I would organize a lottery and give a price to the one who makes the best suggestions for improvement of synergy and team creativity.
Appropriate / / Not Appropriate

I would not care. A leader has to lead and not to listen.
Appropriate / / Not Appropriate

I would first talk to my spouse and ask her/him what to do.
Appropriate / / Not Appropriate

I would fire anyone who contradicts my orders.
Appropriate / / Not Appropriate

Effective Self-Management

Rogotasc is a simple facilitation tool for effective self-management which adds on to leadership qualities and skills on the level of daily and weekly time management, prioritizing, self-definition and goal setting. The term is a composite of the following ingredients:

▸ Roles

▸ Goals

▸ Tasks

▸ Schedule

In one word, *Rogotasc* is a planning tool that is based upon your goal setting and in accordance with your values. Let me explain. Unlike other management or leadership approaches I do not favor daily scheduling.

When we schedule daily, we too easily get into a hassle and do over-planning. I mean life is not linear. There are sudden changes of schedule, there are appointments cancelled, and so on. Daily scheduling pushes us too much on the management side and it's perhaps too poor from the leadership point of view. Hence, leadership planning is weekly. The week is a natural planning unit.

The ideal time for weekly planning is Sunday. If you sit down and do your weekly planning on Sunday afternoon, visualizing your tasks for the new week, you have the emotional distance needed to schedule your tasks in accordance with your vision statement and your goals. Why should we do that? If we forget about our basic leadership tools such as the *vision statement,* we'll be in a *hassle of priorities.* There are certainly important things to do but there are also things on our agenda that are less important.

Often, if we plan on a daily basis we lack the necessary distance from the situation in order to really prioritize successfully; and *prioritizing* is the essential point of self-management or time-management. So what we do now is first to get clarity what our roles are and then set our goals for our tasks and schedule them on a weekly basis.

Roles and Goals

I understand roles and goals not as separate items on the agenda of leadership, but as intertwined. My goals depend on my roles.

If, for example, I consider to be a parent to be my main role for the coming years, specific goals will flow from this role choice. In the following work task, you are asked to identify *5 different roles* you are currently playing in your life, and then assign a few goals to each of them. Do this in a few seconds, without thinking much about it, rather intuitively.

My Personal Role 1

My personal goals for Role 1 ...

My Personal Role 2

My personal goals for Role 2 ...

My Personal Role 3

My personal goals for Role 3 ...

My Personal Role 4

My personal goals for Role 4 ...

My Personal Role 5

My personal goals for Role 5 ...

Now that you have clarity about your goals, you are ready to start with planning or self-management. Enter in every box of your weekly schedule the following data:

- ▸ The day when the task will have to be done;

- ▸ The task to be carried out;

- ▸ The role of your six roles to be assigned to the task;

- ▸ The goal to achieve with carrying out the task;

▸   The gross amount of time needed for the task;

▸   The importance (priority range of the task.

Please enter your solution in the appropriate boxes for every day and don't forget to structure your input along the lines of the six points previously enumerated.

Your Weekly Schedule

Sunday

My Schedule for Sunday

> Weekly Planning

Monday

My Schedule for Monday

Tuesday

My Schedule for Tuesday

Wednesday

My Schedule for Wednesday

Thursday

My Schedule for Thursday

Friday

My Schedule for Friday

Saturday

My Schedule for Saturday

Real-Life Task

You are asked to take presidency of your local club, church or welfare organization. You are supposed to hold a speech at that occasion. You need to prepare the speech and schedule it in your agenda. The club meeting will be on Thursday evening. Priority ranges are from 1 to 10 (1 being the lowest and 10 the highest priority) How do you schedule? (Please enter the solution in the appropriate boxes for every day and don't forget to structure your input along the lines of the six points previously enumerated.)

Sunday

My Schedule for Sunday

Thursday

My Schedule for Thursday

The Way the Task Will Have to Be Done

Short Description

The Role to Be Assigned to the Task

Short Description

The Goal to be Achieved

Short Description

Gross Amount of Time Needed for the Task

Short Description

Importance and Priority of the Task

Short Description

Solution for 'Enhancing Createamity'

Harsh Competition.

Detrimental to Team Creativity

When there is competition among the team members, they will tend to perceive each other as potential enemies or at least as rivals. This is going to undermine the synergy of the team and may create a cold or even hostile atmosphere in the team.

Spy for the Boss.

Detrimental to Team Creativity

It is certainly detrimental to a team's spirit if one member functions as a spy. As long as this is not discovered, the team may function well on the surface. But on the underlying level, real trust can't be built because there will be a lack of honesty right from the beginning. Once the whole thing comes to be known, the team will be definitely broken off and there is even a danger that the large amount of mistrust and negativity that is then present will impede a new team from functioning at all.

Weekly Meeting.

Not Detrimental to Team Creativity

The amount of time that the team is involved in interaction is not decisive. What is decisive is the *quality and the effectiveness* of the team's interactions.

If the team really is synergistic, it will need a relatively short time to build common denominators and win-win solutions.

Larger Team.

Not Detrimental to Team Creativity

Although it may be challenging for a team, team creativity does not go down the river just because the team expands and gets larger. This is a process of adaptation the team has to go through. The example of Microsoft® Corporation has shown that the transition is possible without hurt if the CEO or direction team knows how to direct and motivate creative teams and creates overlapping functions.

No Knowledge about Families.

Detrimental to Team Creativity.

This question could be answered in either way. It's a bit on the gray line. I would tend to say that if there is no sharing about personal information in the team, there can't be real trust, there can't be real exchange and thus there can't be a real basis for synergy.

Only Email Discussions.

Detrimental to Team Creativity.

This is a classical case where the team is 'put on ice' by an incomprehensive company direction. If communication between the team members is restricted to such an extent, synergy becomes impossible since it requires open-minded and manifold exchange.

Gym and Volleyball.

Not Detrimental to Team Creativity

Such activities are very positive to create synergy in the team. Social activities that are looked forward to are in many Fortune 500 companies one of the keys of their tremendous success.

Team Leader Changed.

Not Detrimental to Team Creativity

This in itself is no reason for the team to become dysfunctional. In the contrary could it happen that the new team leader knows better how to create synergistic teams.

However, it is also true that creative teams are more flexible and support challenges better than non-creative ones.

One Contradictor.

Not Detrimental to Team Creativity

This in itself is no reason for the team to become dysfunctional. In the contrary can such a person stimulate the team to become more proactive and to implement positive changes.

Team Not Open to the Outside World.

Detrimental to Team Creativity

Such behavior shows that the team is fundamentally anxiety-ridden and not open to learn or absorb enriching input from other teams. That means the team is really dysfunctional.

The problem may be with the team director who has to take care that the team doesn't become claustrophobic but remains positive toward the outside. Teams that react the way as described in the example are no teams in reality.

They are bundles of individuals who relate to others only because of their unresolved inner anxieties.

Team Discriminates.

Detrimental to Team Creativity

This behavior is similar to the one of the previous example. Teams that discriminate are *anxiety-ridden* and fear for their external unity which is but a façade. Inside those teams, the members are not 'bonded' emotionally and are rather hostile to each other, which is why, in critical situations, they project this hostility upon new members or new members who are 'different.'

No Good Bye.

Not Detrimental to Team Creativity

This in itself is no reason for the team to be dysfunctional. In the contrary can such behavior show that the team members feel basically secure with each other and do not need 'formal politeness' to keep up with their synergy. Much here also depends on the cultural set and setting.

CEO is Friend.

Not Detrimental to Team Creativity

This in itself is no reason for the team to become dysfunctional. In the contrary can the 'hot line' to the CEO encourage the team to work harder and produce better results than other teams, for they can be sure that 'the boss will know about it.'

Authoritarian Leadership.

Detrimental to Team Creativity

To treat human beings like 'order-receivers' is not the best and certainly no creative approach to team leading. Such kind of behavior puts off the most willing of collaborators because every person with a potential will tend to feel low and degraded if they are not valued in his or her deepest person.

Genius brings New Ideas.

Not Detrimental to Team Creativity

This in itself is no reason for the team to become dysfunctional. In the contrary can such a person awaken the team's sleeping abilities and catalyze new creative processes that enhance synergy in the team.

Solution for 'Becoming a Team Interactor'

There are only 5 right answers from a total of 15 possible answers. What can this fact tell us? Well this fact actually shows that it is very hard *not to be proactive* in a team, and thus rather difficult to block a team's natural dynamic to become involved in synergistic behavior.

Why is that so? When human beings interact with each other, there is a high probability that their energies get hotwired with each other, except in the case that one or more interactors block the communication by exhibiting—

▸ Negative feelings;

▸ Poor self-esteem;

▸ Communication inability;

▸ Negative intentions;

▸ Corrupted attitude;

▸ Poor trust level.

Sabotage the team.

Inappropriate for the team interactor.

That was obviously a trap question. However, some people do exactly that, yet without bad intention, simply by gossiping or otherwise undermining the team's general trust level through inappropriate or unworthy behavior.

Solution focus.

Appropriate for the team interactor.

This strategy is the classical example of how to get a hassled-up team into a new positive drive. Give people a dream and they will dream together, says the adage. And it's true. There is no stronger incentive to get together as when there is a common goal to strive for, a common problem to solve, a common vision to pursue.

Have the team review former decisions.

Appropriate for the team interactor.

Although this way of doing requires tact, it is a possible action toward the team's self-identity and self-esteem. Reviewing former decisions is something people like to do because there is something tangible to talk about, something which has already delivered results. The process of reviewing however should be *careful, positive and encouraging,* not harshly criticizing which could make things worse.

Tell everybody around about the team.

Inappropriate for the team interactor.

Even if done with good intention, gossiping and verbiage when 'out of the door' undermines trust in a group or community. Gossiping quickly turns into finding the culprits or risking the big mouth or other negative human expressions. It hardly ever delivers anything positive.

With diplomacy and tact getting team involved.

Appropriate for the team interactor.

This is certainly a technique that works. It is the careful approach that produces long-term results. However, there is one restriction to this answer. The team leader would be in a *more appropriate position* than a team member for this task. Much depends in practice on the personalities of the people involved.

Play the contradictor.

Inappropriate for the team interactor.

While contradicting might in some cases have a stimulating effect on the group, it generally creates *confusion and insecurity* among the team members. This is so much the more the case when the devil's advocate is played by one of the team members. (If the team director plays this role, it may be more easily accepted). One of the reasons that contradicting undermines synergy is that the true reasons for contradicting are never really obvious to others. Since it is seldom that a contradictor wants but to stimulate with having the best outcome for the team in mind, it is generally suspected that s/he acts for selfish reasons or just for showing off. And such an attitude definitely acts counter to synergy.

Invite the team to a TV-evening.

Appropriate for the team interactor.

This is a generally approved form of team interaction. While it could be argued that this role does fit more for the team director, it is more often than not readily accepted by groups when one group member offers his or her house for a meeting or a leisure activity. However, if the person uses the occasion for showing-off, playing out the ego-trip or starting hot debates about daily issues, the effect may be negative for team synergy and/or may lead to a later isolation of the concerned team member.

The nice guy attitude.

Inappropriate for the team interactor.

While it is recommendable to *first listen to the others* and to be friendly in every team interaction, it is certainly destructive to team synergy if one team member stays completely closed up.

This is so because such behavior creates the strong impression of either mistrust or lack of involvement both of which is considered as rather antisocial behavior. It is different when the person is shy and opens up later on. In fact, people have a fine sense of the difference between initial shyness, on one hand, and lack of commitment, on the other. Generally it is true that the engaged, committed but speaking-up kind of person is more readily accepted in a group than the aloof type of person.

The Socratic attitude.

Inappropriate for the team interactor.

While it can be stimulating to play the Socrates for tackling problems from unusual perspectives, this role, if ever, is more appropriate for the team director.

But even then, it is a fact of life that sophisticated mind games bear the danger that team members who are slow thinkers easily feel put off and stop interacting.

The second danger is that the emotional bond (which is often more important than the intellectual understanding) gets lost because communication from the heart is different from purely intellectual communication. Generally speaking, exchange coming from the heart encompasses intellectual exchange, but not necessarily the other way around.

First talk to the team director.

Inappropriate for the team interactor.

This attitude is generally considered as weak, typically exhibited by people who are lacking basic self-confidence and trust. It tends to be associated with a slavish mind.

Persons with this attitude are seldom trusted because they correspond to the image of the official who tries to shift his responsibility up to the supervisor or department head. Today more than ever before this attitude will easily be rejected by the group—and for good reasons!

First listen and understand.

Appropriate for the team interactor.

This is certainly one of the best if not *the* best attitude for every team member to adopt right from the start. It ensures to be well informed about what's actually going on, and for understanding the underlying group dynamics.

Besides, someone who is considered by the group as a good listener is really listened to.

Put posters on the wall.

Inappropriate for the team interactor.

This action certainly looks positive on first sight. And it would certainly be well accepted if it came from the side of the team director.

When a team member exhibits such behavior, however, the effect on the group would be rather awkward. Because it would easily be considered as a way of showing-off or of being pushy. Therefore I strongly disadvise such behavior.

Don't care.

Inappropriate for the team interactor.

This is *one of the worst attitudes,* prone to be rejected by every group. The answer readily given to those people is 'What are you doing here?'

I think there is no doubt that such indifference is considered as *asocial* from the start. Apart from this, it's certainly not the task of the team leader to get the team members basically involved because this feeling of involvement must come straight from the heart of every person and can never be forced upon. Those who don't care are very welcome to leave, and that is the best they can do to the team, and even the company!

First talk to my lawyer.

Inappropriate for the team interactor.

This attitude is similar to non-involvement, with the only difference that here the decision to become involved is delegated to a third party.

It is an attitude that will in most cases meet with rejection or ridicule from the side of the group.

Do nothing.

Inappropriate for the team interactor.

Not much to say about that. The answer of the group would simply be: 'What are you doing here? Get out!'

Solution for 'Becoming a Team Director'

There are only 5 right answers from a total of 15 possible answers. What can this fact tell us? Well this fact actually shows that it is very hard *not to be proactive as a team director*, and thus rather difficult to block a team's natural dynamic to become involved in synergistic behavior. Why is that so? Because when human beings interact with each other, there is a high probability that their energies get hotwired with each other, except in the case that the team director blocks the communication by exhibiting—

- Negative feelings;

- Poor self-esteem;

- Communication inability;

- Negative intentions;

- Corrupted attitude;

- Poor trust level.

Let's now see the answers in detail.

Tell them what to do.

Inappropriate for the team director.

The team leader should enhance personal responsibility and interdependence of all the team members and not treat them 'from above.' He should gradually responsiblize team members by delegating tasks and supervising only the quality of the result, giving an utmost of freedom to the way the person is actually carrying out the task. This implies that the team director should give latitude and confidence to every team member for choosing the right means to carry out tasks, in accordance with their personal skills and personality.

Solution focus.

Appropriate for the team director.

Solution focus is *one of the best ways to build and unify a team.* Through solution focus the team itself becomes focused, and a focused team is almost always an effective team.

Have the team review former decisions.

Appropriate for the team director.

Creating awareness in the team about previous decisions is very constructive. It helps to clear the past, to put things in a new perspective and, most important of all, to awaken in the team its spirit that—

> ‣ It can do things when things need to be done;

> ‣ It can become creative once it is challenged;

> ‣ It has already proven its right of existence.

All of this gives the team the necessary openness and spirit of adventure for engaging creatively in new tasks— which is exactly what a good team director should be after.

Encourage team for small talk.

Inappropriate for the team director.

While there may be a reason to do that in order to make contacts more spontaneously with members of the team and 'listen to the rumors,' it is a potentially dangerous activity. This is so for three reasons:

▸ It can undermine trust more easily than building it;

▸ It may show the team director as somebody frivolous;

▸ It can be perceived by some as a silent intrusion.

Use diplomacy and tact to define creative tasks.

Appropriate for the team director.

The definition and clarification of tasks is important right at the beginning of a new team director's role.

However, it has to be seen that to define or redefine tasks is a subtle and delicate matter. People use to identify with their work or specific tasks and to suddenly relocate them, worse to *relocate them to other tasks without their consent* is highly imprudent and negatively affects the leadership abilities of the team director.

However, if the team director understands to use diplomacy and tact or should I better say respect and human understanding, s/he will be able to position or relocate team members in a way that they themselves perceive the change positively, for example as a promotion or a new creative challenge.

Playing the boss.

Inappropriate for the team director.

While this role may be personally satisfying, it not only undermines the team's trust level, but gradually regresses people back into infancy.

Dictatorship creates codependence and infantile, irresponsible forms of behavior on the side of the followers. Strangely, also on the side of the dictators themselves.

There is actually nobody who really profits from dictatorship; the dictator himself neither as he will quickly feel isolated, lonely and on a level of low energy.

Invite team to children's party.

Appropriate for the team director.

Invitations to one's private home are considered as a sign of friendship and trust. If the invitation is for a child's or children's party, the gesture is considered even more affectionate. It could give opportunity to valuable informal exchange as being around children generally affects people positively and makes them more open and even more creative.

Play the ignorant.

Inappropriate for the team director.

Problems can't be solved when they are hidden or 'swept under the carpet.' A team director who is afraid to talk to his team or is indifferent to the team's needs, demands or problems, is simply at the wrong place.

Strict guidelines and hire-and-fire.

Inappropriate for the team director.

Even if it can be argued that there are situations in human togetherness where so-called 'strict discipline' is appropriate, it is generally infantilizing or regressing people, thereby cutting down their response-ability level.

Strict guidelines as such can at times be appropriate, especially in unstable teams. However, if rules of conduct are secured by severe measures such as setting staff off, they are not perceived by the team as guidelines but as punishments. A wise team director will not play negatively on people's emotions, but stimulate and motivate the team positively.

First talk to company director.

Inappropriate for the team director.

Such a team director will be considered as incompetent from both the director's side as from the side of the team.

In addition, his action is unwise as the team would lose basic trust to him or her supposing the team director lacks out on integrity, or acts toward the team like a spy. I would say this kind of behavior is one of the worst for a team director. Nobody likes secret agents or people who talk 'behind the back.'

First listen and understand.

Appropriate for the team director.

Probably the best of all possible ways of acting as a new team leader. Only positive results can come out of it.

Organize a lottery.

Appropriate for the team director.

Organizing a lottery is one of the good and creative solutions to the problem of building synergy.

I would not care. A leader has to lead and not to listen.

Inappropriate for the team director.

There is not much comment to be made on this attitude. It simply shows someone who has never understood what it means to be a leader.

I would first talk to my wife or husband.

Inappropriate for the team director.

Such behavior is a sign of *emotional dependency* which is detrimental to the capacity to take decisions responsibly and within a sphere of personal autonomy.

This is already basic for self-leading and so much the more for team-leading. People who suffer from a problem with codependence, or from a childhood hangup are generally weak leaders.

I would fire everyone who contradicts my orders.

Inappropriate for the team director.

This is *one of the weakest attitudes* in a leading position. It shows lacking self-confidence or outright incompetence.

Nobody gives trust to such a person, not even, as it's in dictatorships, by force. People can be forced to comply, but they *cannot be forced to trust and bond,* and develop commitment. The best indicator for recognizing a weak leader is to detect if the person *forces decisions upon team members* instead of taking decisions together with them.

Solution of Sample Task

Real-Life Task

You are asked to take the presidency of your local club, church or welfare organization. You are supposed to hold a speech at that occasion. You need to prepare the speech and schedule it in your agenda. The club meeting will be on Thursday evening. Priority ranges are from 1 to 10 (1 being the lowest and 10 the highest priority) How do you schedule? (Please enter the solution in the appropriate boxes for every day and don't forget to structure your input along the lines of the six points previously enumerated.)

Sunday

My Schedule for Sunday

> Preparation of the speech; meditative mind, concentration and quietness. It's difficult to carry out such tasks during a busy week. Even if we plan them on the evenings, after work, experience has shown that most people tend to be tired or worn out or just not in the mood for creative writing. Generally rest is needed for those tasks wherefore we should give them a moment during the weekend, ideally in the morning, on Sundays. (Time : 1 to 2 hours. Priority : 10 because it is an important function to develop leadership skills, it's honorable and it's a good goal)

Thursday

My Schedule for Thursday

> On Thursday morning you should briefly review your speech. The best time for this would be just after awakening because your mind then is still open and receptive. You should read the speech quietly and then close your eyes to impregnate the deep sense of what you said into your mind, rather than the words you used to express it. (Time: 20 min.) Thursday evening before leaving your office you should do the same but more briefly (10 min.). This is for refreshing your memory with what it has been already impregnated in it.

The Way the Task Will Have to Be Done

Short Description

> Creative writing, concentration, preparing yourself for public presentation, reviewing your values and goals, formulating your vision in public.

The Role to Be Assigned to the Task

Short Description

> Something like *Caretaker* or *Voluntary for Human Cause* or *Social Group Leader* or *Social Administrator*.

The Goal to be Achieved

Short Description

> Serving humanity, helping social welfare to progress, work for the common good, care for higher living standard, attack social injustice, etc.

Gross Amount of Time Needed for the Task

Short Description

> 2 hours preparation plus 1 hour reviewing equals about 3 hours in total.

Importance and Priority of the Task

Short Description

> Priority : 10 because it is an important function to develop leadership skills, it's honorable and it's a good goal.

Points to Ponder

▸ In *Chapter Three* I expanded on team interaction and direction, which is today one of the single most difficult things in corporate life. I have seen people of all walks of life, rich and poor, outgoing or introvert, yet for all of them, their relationships in the group were and are the point where they seem to be more or less powerless, incurring large-scale suffering simply as a matter of lacking autonomy, and lacking knowledge about the art of relationship. Relationship is an art, but an art that can be learnt.

▸ The very first and most important step in handling relationships is to develop a stable and structured *self-identity*.

▸ This is brought about through leaving an infantile state of dependency and building true interdependence with others.

▸ To get there, first independence, self-reliance and autonomy need to be built. This sounds very theoretical, but it is eminently practical because most people carry sequels of their accidented or unfinished primary symbiosis in their adult lives, thereby projecting their infantile need for symbiosis and fusion, on others, their partner, their children, and also their associates and business partners.

▸ This is a highly explosive topic in our modern consumer culture. Here, I summarize the process in three simple and clear steps:

▸ Grow from dependence into interdependence;

▸ Leverage positive attitude and win-win;

▸ Relate emotionally to others without getting entangled.

▸ *Dependence* can be described as fusion with others, *Independence* as disconnection from others and *Interdependence* as flexible exchange with others. Nothing but looking at these three sentences, it becomes obvious that the third option is the only creative among them.

▸ Both fusion and disconnectedness are not what the human realm is about. When we talk about the plant realm, we indeed talk about fusion, and symbiosis. But we are not plants, while we can learn some truths from plants; but in matters of relationship, we human beings are closer to mammals and with mammals, and even with birds, we see that once grown up, they leave their nest and pretty much forget about their parents. It seems that in modern consumer culture, it's the other way around, and the older the child grows, the more he or she is entangled with their parents.

▸ This being said, it is certainly a challenging task to go beyond mere self-development and enter the stage of group development, that is, a kind of evolution that is shared in a team so that the growth experience becomes an exciting venture that serves interpersonal communication.

▸ The contemplative, imaginative and literary activities I have offered in this chapter were destined to propel you into sharing your personal growth story with others, be it with your partner, be it with your children, be it with your colleagues at work. The energizing fact is that when you share personal evolution in a company team, not only the participants profit from it, but the company as a whole. This in turn feedbacks and recycles back to the team, which has a highly energizing effect.

▸ But for this to happen, the right interpersonal relationship techniques need to be employed and mistakes and clumsy advances need to be avoided as best as it can. When you are in the role of a team actor, you have a different perception of the process than when you are in the role of the team director. Both positions are interesting and serve your personal growth once you assume to live the experience positively, and with an open mind and heart.

▸ The methods I am suggesting in this chapter were tested both in the corporate setting and in a governmental train-the-trainers setting for the proper formation of civil servants.

Chapter Four

Building Vision

What is Vision?

This is now the place to practice your customized version of what I use to call your *personal vision*. It can be exciting to formulate a *personal vision statement* together with your colleagues, so that the personal vision becomes a collective vision, a group vision, or the vision of a creatively interacting team.

All corporate vision statements are ultimately distillations of the personal vision statements of all participating members of the team.

Vision building is really a prime requirement for the successful running of cutting-edge postmodern organizations around the world and is valid both for private business and governmental organizations.

The secret of success is to let everyone in the company participate in *building the vision* of the organization's successful implementation and market (or governmental) behavior.

Solutions that have been worked out synergistically are 'carried on the shoulders' of everyone who comes to work in the morning. This means that everyone will feel greatly involved and comfortable to contribute to the common good of the whole organism, and not only think of his personal profit.

I have done the whole of this work, from personal to corporate, assisting first individuals and then corporations, and I insist that the personal must come first, and the corporate thereafter. I then began to train the top team members of various organizations in drafting their personal vision statements until the team-based working out of the company vision statement.

Now we will work here exclusively on your *personal vision*, because this practice, to repeat it, is the *foundation of any work on vision on the professional level*. Naturally, when you do not know what your personal vision is, it will be hard for you to formulate your vision as a free-lancer, as a consultant, or if you work for a boss, at your work place.

In every process of integration into a collective body such as a group or organization there is a *functional dialectic* to observe. There are forces in group dynamics that drive us out of our center, or de-personalize us.

Integration in a group is a creative adaptation. It is ideally not total adaptation where the personal characteristics disappear. In a democratic organization the individual is given a *creative space* within which to operate.

More this space is used by the members of the organization, more the organization will benefit and become successful, be it financially, be it in terms of power and social influence and standing.

Now it may become clear to the reader that individuals who have a firm inner value system, a strong character and yet flexibility and friendliness towards others and, first of all, integrity and loyalty for the public cause or common good, will advance very quickly to the top of the organization. Top leadership exactly needs persons with such qualities.

Your Personal Values

Start with identifying your personal values. Here we deal with drafting our *personal vision statement* and find out about our personal values. We collect information first and then finalize our vision statement by actually drafting it in words and layout.

Let's begin and see what you believe are your personal values. Please choose *five values* out of the following list by putting a cross on them with a pen or underlining them. They are the ones you value most, the ones you set on the first place, the values you give the priority. Then, choose five other values:

- Integrity

- Honesty

- Popularity

- Exactitude

- Excellence

- Truthfulness

- Loyalty

- Friendliness

- Friendship

- Cleverness

- Intelligence

- Intuition

- Peace

- Harmony

- Charity

- Truth

- Creativity

- Persistence

- Quality

- Reliability

- Faith

- Contribution

- Wisdom

- Responsibility

- Compassion

- Wit

- Fairness

- Courage

- Health

- Financial Security

- Happiness

Five Favorite Values

These are my five favorite values

Five Other Values

These are my five other values

Your Personal Roles

Next, find out about your personal roles. We collect information first and then finalize our vision statement by actually drafting it in words and layout further down. Envision now the main roles you wish to adopt in your private and professional life. For example, parent can be a role you may want to take, or bank director, or husband, or writer. Make your choice of *five roles* out of the list and submit them, and in addition choose five other roles:

▸ Parent

▸ Coach

▸ Writer

▸ Husband

▸ Sport

▸ Champion

▸ Leader

▸ Film

▸ Star

▸ Sales Manager

▸ Film Director

▸ Actor

▸ Wife

- Master

- Disciple

- Composer

- Painter

- President

- Astronaut

- Programmer

- Administrator

- Caretaker

- Social Worker

- Church Official

- Inventor

- Manufacturer

- Philosopher

- Medical Doctor

- Lawyer

- Pharmacist

- Judge

- Pilot

- Foster Parent

- Civil Servant

- Worker

- Healer

- Astrologer

- Numerologist

- Feng Shui Expert

- Fortune Teller

- Acupuncturist

- Publisher

- Internet Service Provider

Five Favorite Roles

These are my five favorite roles

Five Other Roles

These are my five other roles

Your Positive Characteristics

In this sub-chapter we are going to find out about our favorite characteristics.

We collect information first and then finalize our vision statement by actually drafting it in words and layout.

Please choose *four positive characteristics* that you admire in others and would like to subscribe to or adopt for yourself, either that you think you possess those characteristics already, or that you may want to develop them:

- courageous

- wise

- witty

- compassionate

- intelligent
- harmonious
- truthful
- honest
- sane
- caring
- giving
- warm
- strong
- popular
- unselfish
- helpful
- friendly
- serviceable
- fearless
- powerful
- diplomatic
- creative
- spontaneous
- gregarious

▸ charitable

Next you should consider and choose *four positive characteristics* that you admire in others and would like to subscribe to or adopt for yourself, either that you think you have those characteristics already, or that you may want to develop them.

My Four Favorite Positive Characteristics

These are my four favorite characteristics

Four Other Favorite Positive Characteristics

These are my four other positive characteristics

Your Weaknesses

In this sub-chapter we are going to find out about our weaknesses.

We collect information first and then finalize our vision statement by actually drafting it in words and layout.

Honestly consider your weaknesses here as you will have to acknowledge them later in your personal vision statement. Enter your *three main weaknesses* here.

My three main weaknesses

These are my three major weaknesses

Personal Vision Statement

In this sub-chapter we are drafting our personal vision statement in words and layout. For doing this, you just fill in all the information previously collected and assemble it in your statement in a way in keeping with your personal style.

Please use the form below to correctly and completely draft your PVS so that you can review it any time later on, and revise it through new editions.

Personal Vision Statement (PVS)

To find happiness, fulfillment and value in living, I,

[....] will—

LEAD a life centered around the values of—

[Values]

REMEMBER my main roles in life which are being a—

[Roles]

REVERE admirable characteristics in others such as being—

[Positive Characteristics]

and attempt to implement similar characteristics in my own life.

RECOGNIZE my strengths and develop my talents as a person who is a—

[Other Roles]

HUMBLE myself by acknowledging that I can be—

[Weaknesses]

and constantly strive to transform my weaknesses into strengths.

ENVISION myself becoming a person who is—

[Other Personal Characteristics]

My Personal Vision Statement

Complete Version

Points to Ponder

▸ In *Chapter Four* we did not learn theory but were doing the work, in that case, the work to building vision on both the personal and the professional level.

▸ For that purpose, we were drafting our *Personal Vision Statement (PVS)* with all the ingredients it needs for being effective and powerful.

▸ I hope I have been clear enough to convey that we are not talking here about mere wishful thinking. If a vision statement was only wishful thinking, as some older generation managers believe, it would not range among the set of techniques applied today by Fortune 500 companies around the world.

▸ Contrary to those who are still signed up with the old, rigid, authoritarian leadership paradigm and who are at pains with accepting modern work methods, I can safely say that to work out vision statements at every level of the corporation is *not a cutting-edge method anymore*. It can be called a 'classical' method in the meantime, as it was first introduced already back in the 1960s in the United States, and later in other countries.

▸ In addition, it is important to note that it's an almost impossible task to ask employees to participate in formulating a top team or company vision statement *without first having drafted their own personal vision statement*. Both motivation and commitment for doing vision statements are born with the PVS, as the normal beginner stage. Everybody is first interested to see if 'that works for me,' to conclude 'then it may work also for my company.'

▸ The techniques that I am sharing in this guide, while most of them are born in the corporate setting, are not limited to corporate training, but are serving equally well on the private and personal level. You will be amazed what progress you can book in your private life, and relationships, and your self-employed work life, by applying these simple tools, provided you really put them to work!

Chapter Five

Leading Empowered Humans

Leverage Skills and Positive Attitude

The challenge for everyone of us is to learn how to not only have a positive attitude and practice the principle of *win-win* in any kind of relationships, but also to leverage these skills down in the hierarchy of our company so that many people can benefit from them.

Before I am talking about what a positive attitude actually entails, let us look at its very contrary, a negative attitude. Most people speak about positive thinking only in moments when they are anyway positive, but not in moments they are negative. Now when I use such a statement, and from a scientific perspective, I actually say something that floats in the air. What does it really mean to be 'positive' or 'negative.' Strangely enough, I have never found a book about positive thinking where the author elaborated what 'negative thinking' actually means in practice, and what it is all about?

Many people may actually misunderstand that expression that way, which is why I thought we need to clarify what negative thinking really is. Let me just stay with the examples.

1) Fear/Panic

The first example was a personal situation during the financial crisis back in 2008. It shows a situation of panic and a situation where the person did not build sufficient trust with a bank abroad that cared for his money during a crisis situation. So he withdrew the money and put it in a bank in a country that he considered to be 'safer.' But exactly the contrary of his fears was the outcome.

The country where he had his money initially was not affected by the crisis and the bank in the country where he put his money was careless to manage his portfolio and he lost thirty thousand dollars.

Had the man not panicked because of the financial crisis, and had he left his assets with the first bank, he would not have been affected by the crisis at all. *Panic or fear is certainly a negative reaction.* Experience shows that most rich and super-rich people are positive thinkers, and do not suffer from exorbitant fears.

2) Procrastination

Here the negative emotion is not fear, but procrastination: it was actually a pitiful lack of hope, a lack of endurance, also lacking self-confidence. The man had his money in the bank in a country where he got very high interests on his long-term dollar deposits. This went fine for some years until his private banker told the man he better switch now to invest in real estate as the property market was booming in the country, and sometime in the future, the interest rates for dollar deposits were going to be dropped.

But the man procrastinated. He lacked out on an entrepreneurial spirit, he was afraid of the risk.

While his banker made a huge profit with investing in real estate, the man left his money in the bank. After three years the situation changed and the interest rates for dollar deposits were dropped. The man saw himself faced to invest in real estate in a situation where the peak had been passed and real estate returns were going down again. So he realized that he had missed a big opportunity because of a lack of decision-making and courage.

3) Entanglement

For the third example, I feature a man who was married but was so emotionally entangled with his wife that despite the fact that the wife had another partner and the marriage was definitely broken, he clung to his wife and was unable to separate from her. As a result, he postponed several necessary decisions and prolonged a marriage that was but a mutual role play without affection. During the weekends his wife stayed with her boyfriend, and he was left alone and spent his time working for an academic project.

He thought he was being smart giving his wife so much 'freedom,' but fact was that he was being walked over his feet constantly not only by his wife but also her new partner. As a result, his emotional situation worsened with every day and he began to drink. He felt that he was suffering from something like a 'fear of life,' a constant anxiety that he was unable to get rid off.

One day he found a certain brand of powerful tranquilizers and went to a doctor to get a prescription. The doctor was not aware of the psychic condition of his patient and prescribed a large dose.

The next Saturday morning, the man drank two bottles of wine and took all the tablets, an entire box, when his wife had gone for the weekend. The man wanted to suicide himself.

When his wife entered the studio flat the following Monday morning, she found her husband still asleep in what seemed to be a deep state of coma. She found the empty wine bottles and the remainders of what seemed to be sleeping pills. She called the doctor who came at once, measuring his pulse. 'He is not dead,' he said. 'Your husband is alive, and will probably soon wake up. It's better to let him sleep through this hypnotic condition. After all, it may help him get over his depression.' Destiny was on his side of the man he did not die. The same evening he woke up to what seemed to be a new life. He said to his wife, calmly, and with poise, that he was going to ask for the divorce. His wife nodded silently, and then smiled. She said: 'I knew that you had to get to this point, but I did not want to push you. Now it's done, and perhaps you can accept it all now?' He replied that he was much more happy now, not knowing why, but that somehow his inner condition had entirely changed. He realized with astonishment that his fear of life was gone, and that he was a free man!

Let me now outline what I mean when I talk about a positive attitude and a win-win approach in relationships. Much has been written about positive thought and a positive approach to life. Let me simply state it that way:

 ▸ A positive attitude is a creative attitude in the sense that the status quo is not perceived as unchanging or stagnant, but as a forum for personal evolution;

 ▸ A positive attitude is to see the glass which is half filled with water as a half glass of water. A negative attitude sees the same glass as a glass that is half empty;

 ▸ That's the basic difference. It's the way we look at life, the way we *evaluate* life. Behind our evaluation there is an inner scale on which we measure;

 ▸ This inner measure is our *attitude* that per se is either positive or negative or else is something in between the two extremes;

 ▸ You may have observed that human beings are very different in this respect. In general, in this world and in our times, there are many *more negative than positive people.*

We already have dealt with how to change our inner script. Now, I will give an answer to the question of how to leverage a positive attitude and a win-win approach toward others. This namely depends on how we are *communicating our inner values to others*. We do this all the time, but few of us do it consciously.

The first step is the *firm intention* to irradiate positive values all around us, like an energy radiation, if you will.

We must have built a sufficiently high amount of self-esteem and an inner conviction in the validity of our goals.

In recognizing our difference and building a profound respect for life and other beings, we can get there without too much strife and effort. To repeat it, to radiate goodwill, joy, love and acceptance all around you is the fuel of such an attitude—and it really pays a good dividend!

There are three practical steps for communicating inner strength and values to others:

▸ Read your vision statement once or twice every day;

▸ Practice active and uncompromising forgiveness;

▸ Search always for synergy with others, despite differences.

Leadership in a New Era

It is a world of difference to lead authority-craving un-creative nerds or empowered, assertive, strong and creative individuals.

A leader under the old paradigm just needed to embody the qualities of the *strong father*, and he was basically set. This will be entirely different in the new era, and such an *old-style* leader will rather timely experience to be discarded, simply because an authoritarian, harsh dominator style in leading others is not what really fosters creative deployment, high and very high performance, and self-motivation.

We already saw that conceptually speaking, a servant leader doesn't really fit in the old image of the 'bully on top,' and he or she doesn't need to boast their profile or boost their charisma.

On the contrary, a too-much of throwing their weight around will quickly be perceived as oppressive and 'head-drilling,' and under the new paradigm of global cooperation, dogmatic leadership styles ultimately deserve failure because they are dysfunctional in a networked society.

They are also ineffective, and in the long run may even damage the software of the company, that is, the human resource, the most precious asset a company has.

When leaders recognize the basic premises and quirks of quantum physics and consciousness research, the fact namely that we are all connected, they will more easily become aware that leading basically is nothing but watering flowers; when we recognize that all there is in the universe is *potential*, we see that what a good leader should do is to foster the blooming up and the manifestation of potential, nothing more and nothing less.

Dominant attitudes and judgmentalism do not help in the process of recognizing and localizing potential within the boundaries of the company; only sensitivity and vulnerability can be of use, and smart.

The New Human

Over the last several millennia, most of our religious and philosophical doctrines complacently indulged in the group fantasy of humans being rotten perverse creatures blemished with original sin, who need to be 'reformed' and 're-educated' from the ground up in order to become valuable citizens and a good work force.

This myth about the human nature has created havoc in our relationships, in our social structures, and in our educational systems. It has been taken for granted for too long. In addition, moralism has largely contributed to bestowing a kind of pseudo-validity upon those stories, and thereby elevated them to something like a universal mold that served for the manufacturing of the *good citizen*, as the modern incarnation of the old faulty human.

Unfortunately, our moral apostles and spiritual gurus forgot to consider that such kind of human is not really functional in a networked economy where the individual is validated according to his or her skills, not according to their level of conformity to religious or political systems.

This 'good citizen' has been unveiled by psychoanalysis as the human dummy who elects political tyrants, one who gives consent to holocaust and large-scale genocide, one who is blind to political realities, one who is easy to manipulate and to mislead, one who largely ignores reality outside of the homely nest, and one who can't handle their emotions, being dysfunctional in any kind of group setting, be it in the professional world, or privately, and so on and so forth.

The change of values that will once bring out another vintage of the human was conspicuously not effected by our good and virtuous gurus and saints, not by our saviors and tradition-obsessed noblemen, not by our artist freaks, and not by our rebellious youth, but by *company leaders*, in a step-by-step marathon that is hardly ever seen or portrayed in the media, but that is daily reality in any company around the world. Tell me, where is the responsible and dynamic organization leader who wants humans who:

▸ are stuck in conformity;

▸ are lacking self-knowledge;

▸ are unable to handle their emotions;

▸ are backstabbing others for personal gain;

▸ are fearful and guilt-ridden;

▸ are murky and false;

▸ are unable to assume responsibility?

And yet every *good citizen* can be characterized exactly that way. So my question is: was there ever a visionary, strong, smart and wistful company leader who wanted to have 'good citizens' as his staff? My answer is clearly and decidedly no. And when you realize that, you realize that it's our company leaders, through changing the corporate culture, who have done the first and perhaps even the last step to change humanity as a whole. It was not those who are paid for the job, our religious clergy, for they are too busy with keeping a low profile after all the countless multi-vectorial rapes and robberies of the Church that were being revealed over the last two centuries.

Who is at the frontline of that totality of social change, I am asking? Is it the priests, the monks, the nuns? I know the smart reader will simply laugh here, because *the question is forbidden*. We don't want shame upon our clergy because we all know they have just 'representative' functions, and are otherwise useless.

We all know that it was, if ever, the school principles, universities rectors and corporate leaders who, jointly, have fulfilled this almost superhuman task, and in a very incremental manner, and at very low speed. Because they had no support. The culture was against them, at that time, the religious establishment was against them, the wealth establishment was against them because the latter, in their eternal retrogradation, thought it needed good citizens instead of *functional citizens*. They were not dealing with the human matter, busy with buying and selling their vanity, as a matter of standing. So they knew as little as the clergy about what's really going on in terms of the change of the human from a good citizen to a functional, integrated, responsible and happy citizen. And last not least, the politicians, eternally busy with turning things upside-down that are good and turning things downside-up that are not good, were 'not properly informed,' and thus had an excuse that after all, they were 'not asked for their opinion.'

Did the new human change our leaders? Or did our leaders change the human? What was first, the hen or the egg?

I say that our leaders changed the human, but you are invited to contradict and take the opposite position. Both may have operated in silent synchronicity; it may have been, and is, a *dialectic process*.

And the question is not really important. What is important is to see that it was an *inside* process, which involved the corporate leader, on one side, and the corporate worker, on the other. Both did the work.

Not the priests, not the police, not the politicians. That is the important thing. And it's a good thing, really. That's why an enterprise is called a 'company,' because people there accompany each other, and are giving each other company. Not the family, not the nest, not the marriage, not the political party, not the church, but *company life* is the breeding lot for human progress.

Points to Ponder

▸ In *Chapter Five* I expanded about leading new humans, being a leader under the new paradigm. Being a leader in the new age will be a totally new leadership experience for there is a *fundamental difference* between leading authority-craving and dependent souls or empowered and create-able humans! The difference is so deep that I say a leader who hasn't been prepared for that change, will simply not be able to lead those people, and he or she will be discarded. Hence the need for leaders to upgrade their inner software, and really go with the paradigm changes that are occurring right now, rather than going against them.

▶ We have seen that vision is not enough, but a necessary first step that should ideally be followed by leveraging skills and a positive attitude toward building a true win-win in every situation, and in every relationship.

▶ Let me clarify what *win-win* means. It does *not* mean you are going to be the proverbial doormat. It means that you see both your interests and those of your interlocutory, and that you share and communicate with empathy, and a positive intention. It does *not* mean you become the savior of anybody or 'Mr. Nice Guy'—not at all. The simplest explanation is perhaps to see that for creating true win-win, you need to build an *expansive worldview*, which is based upon *positive values*. Positive values can namely be shared, and communicated, which makes that they become wires that connect people.

▶ There are three preliminary conditions you should meet before you can expect that you are able to build true win-win with others. You should—

▶ Read your vision statement once or twice every day;

▶ Practice active and uncompromising forgiveness;

▶ Search for synergy with others, despite differences.

▶ For *building synergy*, practicing forgiveness is essential. We all carry sequels from our early experiences in life. Who has ever gone through life unhurt? I have studied the lives of very successful people for several years and can say that, with few exceptions, they have been hurt worse than you and me, or they have experienced major reject, or they have been plagued by disease. The one single faculty these people have over most others is that they can put the past behind, that they have enough motivation and enthusiasm to restart, to relaunch their lives tomorrow morning at 8 am! It's really nothing else than that.

▸ Call it a stoic mindset, call it persistence, call it a jack-in-the-box behavior, it works! It works in the sense that it avoids us to become bitter and full of resentment, for two things happen when you turn bitter: people will begin to avoid you and positive coincidences tend to happen less. Fate works with those who are committed to life, not to those who complain and give up. And as we are all similar in this respect, it's draining vital energies to be around a bitter and resentful person, and as this is really a matter of energy exchange, not a matter of morality; you can't complain about it, and you cannot argue 'Oh, these people are bad friends; good friends will stay true also to a friend who grows bitter and negative.' No, they won't, in the long run, for everybody has to care for their own happiness first. That is simply so.

▸ For building synergy, it's absolutely essential to put the past behind, and to heal the old wounds through periods of inner work, introspection, contemplation or meditation. You can also put it in the terms used by Don Miguel Ruiz, in his 'Toltec' books, when you meet a new person in your life, forget about your story, put your story behind you, so that you can see that person as she really is, and not through the glasses of your own story.

▸ True response-ability is built upon inner freshness, so is synergy. It can't be built upon resentment and a generally negative worldview that takes every opportunity to complain about 'my bad life' or 'all those bad people.' When you see that people like Helen Keller have overperformed despite the fact of having been severely underprivileged in some way, you see that the human potential is stronger than any possible defeat—provided you *use* it.

▸ It's a comfortable myth to think that these people were 'special natures' and had 'special inner strength.' No, we all have this strength, but it needs to be activated, and it's activated through commitment to life and growth, not through commitment to death and defeat.

▸ That also means leaders have to read and learn, and learn again, to know the fundamental laws of the cosmos that have been largely expanded under the pulpit of *quantum physics*; some of these laws even have been obsoleted, such as the old belief the universe was a clockwork and the human body functioned like a machine, or that nature could be observed in a 'passive, uninvolved' manner, while in truth, the observer is always entangled with the object of observation.

▸   New leaders will have to recognize that the good human is not the 'good citizen' in the old sense, the stiff uncreative 'homo normalis' who projects all their inner blind spots upon others, and minorities, racial, ethnic, sexual or other, but the empowered and lucid human who accepts self and others, and who has gained the true insights about life through acquiring self-knowledge.

Chapter Six

The New Values

The Value of Systemic Thinking

The *Aquarius Age* has been defined as a new era the onset of which would date around the year 2600, some astrologers date it around the year 2060.

Hence we are not yet really within the Aquarian cosmic cycle, properly speaking; it has to be understood, however, that cosmic cycles that extent over millennia (the *Pisces Age* reigned for 2000 years) will never make a sudden transition. Instead, there is a long prelude and an equally long afterlude for each of those cycles.

Currently we are in an interesting state of ambivalence, a time of transition where we feel the effects of the new age beginning to manifest, but where, at the same time, the values of the old paradigm are still in place, and are even defended with quite some emphasis.

The present trend for fundamentalist solutions in social and legal matters are an example for how the old paradigm defends its existence with quite some drama. But fact is that the social and collective regard of these phenomena, be they something very much present in our daily news, will shift over time.

Astrologers have been especially proficient with contributing to the public discussion information about the *specific new paradigms* the Aquarius Age will inaugurate in the world. This is rightly so since the very notion of *Aquarius* is derived from the Zodiac. But this is not the only reason why astrology plays today a predominant role in modern society. In my view, the main reason why astrology is today a serious discipline of social and political research and even prediction is its *cyclic* way of thinking.

The Zodiac teaches us the truth that nothing in life is a single isolated event but that all is interconnected and cyclic, and therefore subject to repetition.

Astrologers have during all times emphasized the high importance of *cyclical thinking* as opposed to linear thinking. The Aquarius Age will be an era in which humanity is going to reconsider and reformulate all of its fundamental life paradigms. Already now it can be seen that in progressive scientific circles the emphasis is a movement away from linear and toward cyclic or *nonlinear thinking*.

The *Pisces Age*, which we are currently leaving behind, is associated with the 12th House of the Zodiac and thus with the collective, as opposed to the individual, with mass obsessions, and focus on illness instead of health, with secrecy and taboo instead of free speech, segregation instead of integration. It is associated with *Neptune* as the ruler of Pisces and thus with water and emotions in their raw, non-integrated form.

The Aquarius Age is associated with the 11th House of the Zodiac and thus with friendship, communication beyond borders, and sharing ideas without regard to cultural or political limitations. It is associated with Uranus and with the element Air emphasizing *electronic communication* as one of the most central issues in the Aquarius Age.

The Value of Individuality

Let us have a look now at the essential differences in the social and political paradigms that are associated with *Pisces Age*, on one hand, and the *Aquarius Age*, on the other.

Pisces Age	Aquarius Age
linear, dogmatic, mechanistic thinking	cyclic, functional, systemic thinking
group over individual	power of the individual and groupings
uniformity, dogmatism, tyranny	diversity, democracy, shared power
fundamentalism, absolutism	functionalism
authority and hero worship	self-power
obedience to leaders	obedience to self
mass education, alphabetization	individualized education
mass media, mass manipulation	media on demand, media choices
lack of identity and spirituality	high identity, self-chosen spirituality
lack of autonomy for the young	high autonomy for the young
high cultural uniformity	high cultural diversity

codependence, narcissism	emotionally integrated sexuality
locality, provinciality	non-locality, globalism, universality
macro-industry	micro-industry
environmental pollution	environmental consciousness
hierarchical and pyramidal structures	flat and neuronal structures
political opacity	political transparence
regional and national values	global values
discarding out, segregating	embracing, integrating
mind-body split	mind-body harmony
accumulation, agglomeration	diversification, recycling
minorities considered as nuisance	minorities considered as enrichment
habitual career choices valued	unusual career choices valued
the neurotic, compulsive character	the genital, flexible character

As already mentioned, the trend under the Aquarius Age will be away from collectivism and toward individualism, away from standard doctrines 'for all' toward more freedom for setting and living our own personalized standards and ways of life. The regard of the state upon the citizen will largely shift. While for the authoritarian state the citizen was a subject, for the new Aquarian state, the citizen is a *customer*.

The Aquarius Age will provide the individual with a greater sphere of self-expression and more options for associating with peers and groupings that pursue similar goals, even if those goals largely differ from the opinions or the lifestyle of the average individual. There will definitely be more space and recognition for *alternative life styles*. The influence of social and political bodies over the individual will decrease and become smoother and more subtle. Political rulership will adopt more of a *caretaking* nature and a kind of creative partnership with the people under the rule. The leadership paradigm will change from leadership to *stewardship* or *servant-leadership*.

The fact that the 11th House is opposite the 4th House shows that tradition will play an important role in the Aquarius Age, however in a form of assimilation into existing lifestyles or in the form of acquiring wisdom from the past, and not directly through the attempt to restore old and outdated ways of living, and not by the imposition of those traditional values. It's not an overlay pattern, but an *integrative pattern* that the Aquarius Age fosters.

In the *Pisces Age* we see tradition often as a way to justify repression or even tyranny; typically, tradition-holders and tradition-seekers are politically right wing and do all they can to *sabotage* the upsurge of a truly pluralistic society.

The Aquarian thinker is deeply concerned about this distorted way of looking at tradition. In Aquarian culture, tradition will be valued as a useful school about human behavior, and for acquiring insights from this source for bringing about more wistful solutions in the future.

The Value of Social Diversity

Socially, the Aquarius Age brings us a society that is highly complex and highly parceled but in which every individual has a higher chance to find a viable space and protection as well as social contact in interest circles of the most various kinds.

Global structural changes will force traditionally oriented business people to change and be more flexible for implementing new and integrated solutions.

Economies are likely to crash if they are unable to do the structural changes needed that globalization requires. New ways for financing projects of global dimensions will be found. It is highly doubtful that the world economy is going to be maintained on the sole basis of a paper currency such as the dollar. There will be challenges that question the existing system to make it safer and more adapted to our networked international business world.

Speculation in rewarding new business models and novel technologies will bring further challenges to the system since those endeavors, when carried out over longer periods of time and large scale bring the money flow all over the world into previously unheard-of streams. Various experts have alerted us that financial conglomerates located mainly in the United States have reached the size of major state budgets. If these large amounts of capital are not used wisely, they could bring the world economy in a chaos point situation of real danger.

These dangers are a result of the *irresponsibility* that has been systematically bred by the authoritarian and monopolistic social and economic policies of the *Pisces Age*.

Organizations such as the Christian Church, founded under the sign and the symbolism of Pisces, have through their power games manipulated, unresponsibilized, even infantilized the masses to such an extent that the common man is currently not in state to really discern right from wrong or good from bad as far as global policies in economy, justice and social welfare are concerned. This is also so because the information flow today has assumed such gigantic proportions that only professional media experts can channel it and provide information that is even remotely accurate. Yet, it is a fact that media multinationals have shown to use their expertise *mainly for manipulating information* rather than presenting raw information.

As a result, the individual, while believing to know more with every coming year, knows actually *less of what's really going on* in the world. In addition, organized religion and ideologies have all shown their destructiveness breeding among human beings separation, segregation, antagonism, arrogance, hatred, jealousy and war.

However, the transparence so typical for the Aquarius Age will gradually disempower the worldwide truth-holder conglomerates and emasculate their imperialistic monopolies and multi-vectorial favoritism that enriches a tiny worldwide oligarchy beyond all measure, while leaving hundreds of millions of people mentally, materially and spiritually impoverished.

On the other hand, new global business opportunities will arise for those who build on freedom and democracy and who listen to the true needs of the masses.

On the other hand, companies that build on privileges or outmoded traditions, a blown-up self-image or that adhere to undemocratic or even tyrannical forms of leadership will be surprised how quickly and effectively the new era will literally wipe them off the surface of international business. The highest reward will be for those who ultimately serve the customer and who have built a service-oriented business model that empowers the consumer, that is transparent, that gives options and that is constant over time.

Personal relationships will go new ways in the Aquarius Age. The house axis 11 — 4 can also be seen as the axis young-old which means in social terms that there will be more communication between the different age segments of society. Relationships and even marriage will be more easily considered okay when partners differ in age.

The Value of Permissiveness

There will be more rights for children and the youth, also in terms of social engagements. Young people will more easily be allowed to move to other places on their own or to engage in relationships with partners of their choice.

The *Aquarius Age* will bring the real changes because the present new generation needs to be grown up to implement them. There will be more rights for elders, too, and a larger consciousness about how important the wisdom is that we receive from smart elders and how important it is that children and old people join for spending time together.

Many projects to enhance the communication between the different age groups have been implemented in the last years, in the United States, Canada, Europe and Australia.

In France, for example, the courageous projects of child psychoanalyst Françoise Dolto have transformed suburban flat areas into places of exchange and communication between children and the elder, and those projects were acclaimed.

The Aquarian man or woman will refuse social collaboration when personal freedom is not granted by society. This new citizen will more easily than before become a social reformer or even revolutionary. This also means that many of the existing forms of social police and denunciation that are undermining personal freedom and trust between people will be abandoned for allowing humanity to develop into a more trustful state of togetherness.

It will be seen that peace can only be based upon freedom, trust and the self-power of the individual, and not upon ruthless competition, tyranny and persecution.

The Value of Boundless Self-Expression

All great inventions, throughout human history, have been motivated and initiated by frustration, the frustration about something lacking in our life, the dissatisfaction that an obvious need of many people at a specific point of time was not met. This is true not only for the invention of the light bulb, but for a whole lot of other inventions that belong to our surroundings and make out our daily life.

The interesting thing about inventions is their revealing us lots about the human nature. When one human being invents, millions of others, who have the same unfulfilled need, just accept that faulty reality, and remain uncreative. It is the one person or a handful of people who sense the need and bring about what so many not even dream of. We can indeed observe historically that human progress was pretty much the merit of individuals, and much less of groups.

This is interesting because it goes along with another phenomenon. If you observe a group of people confronted with the same need, you will see that always the majority is either content with what is, the status quo, or although not content with it, unable or anxious to change it. It's always one individual or a handful who dare to be dissatisfied and take action towards change. *Therefore we have pioneers.* And therefore dissatisfaction is the very seed, and the bliss of progress.

All of you who were at the point to publish a book, audio book or music and encountered the deep frustrations every writer or musician is confronted with, will understand me when I say that *publishing, today more than ever before, is a channeling in the wrong sense.* Of course, I am talking about the traditional form of publishing, the one which is done by large worldwide publishing houses, companies whose business is the commercial exploitation of sharing.

Publishing is basically sharing, sharing of information or of an aesthetic feeling, sharing of a lifestyle, of experiences. What is often overlooked today is that there is a deep ethical foundation in publishing. Democracy is only thinkable with a continuous flow of information reaching potentially everybody. Publishing also involves the risk to be criticized for one's opinions. This in turn means that publishing requires from the publisher a certain amount of courage. When Gutenberg printed the Bible, his motivation was one of sharing, and not one of making money or a business with publishing. I contend that publishing is a *direct outflow of democracy* and at the same time important for the functioning of a democratic society.

The Internet began as a computer-experiment for some military folks and then developed into a gigantic publishing company. The funny thing about this company is that it has no director and no management team and is self-organized and auto-regulated. Some cynics said once the Web was like a horde of monkeys yelling at each other, and that it therefore had no or very little chance to survive as a serious communication highway. However, the negativists were, as so often, not heading right with their pessimistic outlook; today the Internet is prospering as an alternative publishing network.

There are reasons why people want to change certain things, or why they want to change a whole business, a whole industry, and even an entire history. There are manifest reasons, but these reasons are not materialistic, not greed-related in the first place. This is perhaps not always so, but with the Internet, it's surely the case. The reasons are related to personal power and to the ideal of *total communication* between human beings. And that is new. It's new because formerly we were thinking more locally and less globally, we were much more tightly held by our leaders and our militaries, by our flags and our national myths and identities, and we were much more tightly held within the borders and boundaries of our national universes. While now the world has become a village.

We still have national borders, we still have flags, we still have militaries, of course, but we are going to *change the thinker* behind those things, those institutions, and those daily realities. And this thinker, somewhere somehow, has found out that he or she is *more* than a thinker, and that there is more than thinking. We have found out that it's nicer to share thoughts than to think more. We have found that it's even nicer to share thoughts and art, and music, and this beyond our national borders and our national mentalities. We found that all this has somewhere somehow something to do with *love*, and that it's love that is the ultimate motivation of this crazy network that we call the Internet.

And with that new vision, we look at traditional publishing. And we see the traditional publishing situation is such that creative new ways of publishing are most of the time obstructed by the fact that the publisher is profit-oriented and wants to make sure that the book is sold, instead of making sure that the book is *shared*. This situation makes it gifted writers sometimes very hard or even impossible to 'get through' and find the way to their audience. There are many books that were refused again and again and finally ended up for weeks or months on bestseller lists. One famous example is the book *Zen or the Art of Motorcycle Maintenance* by Robert M. Pirsig, one of the most important philosophical books of our times, and which yet was refused by one hundred twenty publishers!

One can only admire the persistence of the author who approached the 121st publisher who, however reluctantly, accepted publishing. This book rapidly sold as a world bestseller and was translated in I don't know how many languages.

My point is that the Internet or, more generally, electronic publishing is a new form of information distribution, and follows different principles than the traditional publishing industry.

To publish on the Internet has several major advantages. The Web is free of the profit filter built in traditional publishing. A natural selection is made through the interest publications find among users. The Web is a living system which grows naturally and is ruled by more subtle laws and customs than the traditional publishing landscape.

These generally unwritten laws are similar to the very foundations of life. This is not astonishing since the Web grew outside the boundaries of century-old conventions. The Web is a landscape where everybody gets a chance to move in and where everybody who pursues literary or musical interests can learn and grow. And where every-body can build and revise publishing strategies, provided they channel their stuff, find the right outlets and do their online marketing.

And when you fail in one of these tasks you probably will not sell your book or audio CD. But that is a different pair of shoes compared to the often senseless rejection en-countered time and again with publishing multinationals that follow *established success strategies* and are much more biased by hidden prejudice than they would ever admit. It's different to fail with your own web publishing, because it *feels* different. There is no shame connected to it.

The Value of Global Cooperation

It seems to me that human intelligence which created the Internet is fundamentally different from all what we had before in human history. The interesting fact about it is that not one man or woman has created it, but many, often simultaneously cooperating from different points of the globe. The Web was thus perhaps the first really effective global institution we have created.

And that is why, among other reasons that I believe the Internet will grow beyond an information highway to be-come a political highway as well. When we compare the Internet with another global institution, the United Na-tions, there are at least two striking differences.

The United Nations was a creation of states, at a gov-ernment level, and not something growing from the base layer of societies. The privileges or advantages that the UN provides were primarily intended for the *principi*, the former kings or rulers, and later for the nation states. Let us not forget the fact that for the protection of the individual, international law still provides only a minimum standard.

Human rights and the rights of minority populations are protected *only within the range of special pacts or agreements*, such as the international conventions against torture, yet the nation states are free to join these international agreements or not.

The second, perhaps more important point of difference is that the United Nations, after their creation, have pretty much split into regional power groups. It's not a coincidence that the European Community (EU) was another branch of the same tree, coming out of vision that people like Woodrow Wilson and, much earlier, even philosophers like Rousseau and Kant had about the future of a united world. At the same time, *European Integration* was pouring wine into the water of the original idea of a Community of Nations that is truly global.

This may sound provocative. Yet we touch here a mystery that goes beyond all what we have observed hitherto on the globe, something that is like a new gospel, a new power, and a new global village for all. So, to put it clearly, the Internet is the *first international organization* that really works in the sense of *res publica*, as the old Romans called political matters. And in that sense, as a forum for the public cause, the Internet really is *functional*.

Minorities, for example, be they racial, political or sexual, are effectively propagated through the Web. The police laws of most countries can prohibit minorities from gathering as long as gatherings take place within local boundaries. But the police cannot legally control them when these gatherings are held online. Since Web meetings are virtual, they do not fall within those laws. As a result it can be said that the Web created more democracy and freedom of speech.

However, this freedom also means that we have to use it responsibly. If we allow people to abuse of it, we jeopardize our newly gained privilege.

International fundamentalism, secret services, right-wing movements, misguided groupings and a large mass of frustrated and negative individuals only wait for the chance to exert a tight control over the Web so as to install new and hitherto unknown forms of totalitarian government and rulership. The only effective way to prevent this from happening is that we exert responsible self-control in all forms of online publishing and virtual communication. This implies that we have to become conscious of the value that is linked to freedom and to simple and unprejudiced human communication.

Instead, people seem to ask for more regulation and strict guidelines for conduct on the virtual space. This is however within the old paradigm. It means to restrict freedom once again because a certain amount of frivolous people are unable to use it responsibly. If we want to avoid this result, we have only one choice, either to provide organizations with set regulations inviting people to become members for set purposes and to limit communication to set purposes and for set interests or topics, or to change the paradigm. What is presently taking place on the Web is the first alternative. It means basically to create cages for people who have not learned to conduct themselves properly outside of those cages, and in full freedom.

Human history was an up and down of times of more and less freedom. But at all times people have searched for cages because they were afraid of freedom or abused of it to the detriment of all.

However, it's not that difficult to live in wild life. While nature basically regulates itself automatically, by a process called *self-regulation.*

I believe self-regulation, which has been found by systems research to be one of the most basic and most functional ingredients of living systems, will become a social and even a political value.

The Value of Self-Regulation

If we respect ourselves and others from a basic inner attitude that forms part of a new paradigm in human togetherness, we do not need organizations that restrict our freedom, nor rules of conduct, for we will innately engage in the right and appropriate forms of behavior for our largely enhanced ways and forms of communication.

Sounds like Utopia? Let's see now together what implications both paradigms, the old and the new, have for our further human evolution in general, and the evolution of the Web, in particular.

The Old Paradigm

The old paradigm represents a system of beliefs that starts from the premise that humans are basically enemy to each other and therefore use deceiving means and strategies in order to communicate. Most governments, still today, adhere to this belief system, which may be called the belief in 'the negative human.'

Typical for the old paradigm is a range of prejudice and phantom beliefs among people belonging to an *in-group* regarding those belonging to an *out-group*. All these beliefs render communication ineffective and, in extreme cases, impossible. We should always keep in mind that war among humans is only possible from the moment communication has halted or has been undermined by phantom beliefs and superstitions.

The old paradigm is deeply conditioned by the *scarcity mentality*, the belief that nature provides only for a certain number of individuals leaving deprived all others, and this despite the fact that everybody who has observed nature clearly sees that one of the basic patterns of nature is *abundance*, and not scarcity. However, the adepts of the scarcity mentality continue to plague the rest of humanity with their negativism, their endless skepticism, their Cartesian reductionism and their total lack of natural spirituality, thus being *responsible for the perpetuation of the old paradigm.*

These people are typically advocating protection, guidance and security when asked for engaging in communication with others, be it in virtual space or in real life. They consider people as 'strangers' who have not qualified to be friends, associates or at least acquaintances. The qualification of a person as a stranger means that the person is potentially dangerous.

The underlying belief these people share is that the world was a hostile battlefield of conflicting interests and desires, probably simply because their own inner life represents such a battlefield of conflicting interests and desires and that they have never found a way to experience inner peace.

Second, these people tend to believe in *Darwinism*, seeing in all human competition an element of the survival of the fittest. As a result of their dominant belief system, the adepts of the old paradigm maintain virtual and real borders and frontiers in the world, intelligence services, armies and other destruction devices because their main defense mechanism is aggression.

In order to communicate, the adepts of the old paradigm gather within set organizations for set purposes, subscribing to set rules of behavior that fundamentally restrict their freedom. They justify their sacrifice of freedom with any pretended gain in social and political security through the big brothers and insane weaponry reservoirs they have created. Unaware of the illusion they are victim of, they strive to give more and more power to those big brothers, thus jeopardizing in the long run the human condition and human survival.

The New Paradigm

The new paradigm represents a set of beliefs which basically admits that humans are made to be friends and brothers to each other. It is shared by a minority of enlightened spiritual teachers, healers, artists and a tiny group of *systems researchers,* and it may be called the belief in 'the positive human.'

The new paradigm posits that as nature is based upon basic self-regulation, all human organization should integrate self-regulation, in all areas of life. Adepts of the new paradigm question why humans react aggressively or with hostility to everything new or unknown, and tend to be more open and communicative in situations that provide doors to the unknown.

Typical for the new paradigm in communication is the attitude to potentially welcome every possible new encounter, be it with representatives or forces opposite to one's own culture or conditioning, thus considering unforeseen experiences as challenges and chances for growth and evolution.

Adepts of the new paradigm can be recognized by *integrity,* their *courage, curiosity, openness* and a *generally adventurous spirit* which considers every human interaction at its root as a great potential chance for love, harmony, understanding and mutual help. It is the adepts of the new paradigm who have created the wonderful new jungle that we call the Internet, although at the present moment the representatives of the old paradigm seem to dominate and control its general landscape.

Adepts of the new paradigm equally question the necessity to join large organizations for maintaining power within the collective. They rather value the individual to such extent that they tend to generally question the institution of organizations that regulate and channel human encounters thus demonstrating more trust for spontaneous human relations within an unorganized gray area of human interaction.

Adepts of the new paradigm therefore are more open to unusual or unforeseen aspects of human relations, be they on an intellectual, psychological, artistic or sexual level. In my opinion, the most important trait of adherents of the new paradigm is their general openness to *restructure human relations* in accordance with all lessons we have collectively learned from the past, with the ultimate goal to enhance human happiness and welfare, personal and societal prosperity and quality of life in the future.

Adherents of the new paradigm are generally grateful for new possibilities of human interaction and they tend to value the Web as a precious new tool and adventure that has its major advantage not on a commercial or economical, but on a purely human level. For these reasons the adepts of the new paradigm are usually very busy learning, using and teaching all the features the Web offers us for creating new forms of human interaction and exchange.

Among them are the geniuses who treasure the holy grail of the Web, the highest vision about the Web as one of the most important features of life in future centuries.

Although constantly exposed to criticism and typical modern-day skepticism, these people build on the positive image they maintain about life, themselves, others and humankind and thus help us all to create the foundations of a better world.

On the Web, presently, the adherents of the new paradigm represent a small minority of intellectuals who are, unfortunately, not yet really organized. They tend to fight single and isolated wars within the fields of their specific interests and occupations. One of the reasons they actively engage in providing publishing opportunities to others on the Web, on a non-profit basis, is that they set out to practically realize their high humanitarian vision of the Web.

Without a doubt it is and will be the adepts of the new paradigm who are actively involved in the further evolution of the Web and new forms of media such as interactive TV, and developing high-level edutainment for a growing amount of humans who seek their personal evolution outside of set organizations and ideologies.

The Value of Political Transparence

Now, let's shift our perspective from the economical to the political and have a closer look at that daring idea of the Web becoming, perhaps not too far in the future, a real *international organization and political forum* of all peoples in the world. We know from the development of the European Union (EU) that the political union is very difficult to realize, and in fact the EU is far from being a political union with all what this would involve for its member states.

The reason is probably that so much trustbuilding is required for a large number of people agreeing on implementing new systems of government or conceding national powers to a supranational organism.

The United Nations is a striking example for how *not to do it correctly*. They were from the beginning set to implement a political unification with, in the future, ideally, a world government. However, the anxieties were and are so high that the courageous goals were pursued less than half-heartedly. The end result was that bad compromises were made, compromises that really were compromising the whole idea and led to an absurd reality which counts as its major fact the largest bureaucracy in the world, engendering an irresponsible waste of resources.

But let me ask, where is the Web heading? You may object that it is too far-fetched to admit that the Web could eventually bring about what both the European Union and the United Nations did not achieve: a world community, a union of nations, of peoples. How can?

If we take a closer look at this seemingly Utopian idea, we see that there is a fundamental difference between the European Union and the United Nations, on one hand, and the Web, on the other, in their respective ways to realize this global union of peoples. The difference is the fact that the Web begins at the basis whereas all other present international organizations began at the top. Let me explain.

On the Web, masses of people from different cultures get into communicating with each other, first for research or academic purposes, then for business, the exchange of goods and services, and eventually for simply getting to know each other, looking at one another's blog, learning from each other, communicating basic needs, feelings and opinions. The trend is that the Web becomes every day more a meeting place for a *large variety of people* communicating for a *large variety of purposes*. While in the beginning the user had to write out every single command, with the graphic interface of the World Wide Web things became really simple and intuitive. In the meantime, also nonliterate people are able to write: they'll just talk and the computer will write for them.

I already pointed out that existing international organizations, despite the fact that they were instituted to unify peoples, have begun their work with the top classes of society, the rulers, kings and later the sovereign states, and not really seven billion individuals.

If we build a house from the roof, forgetting about its foundation, its basis, the house will crash before it is ready.

This is the true reason why neither the European Union nor the United Nations accomplish in reality what they have been created for: it's simply because they were established as *roof structures with a pitiful lack of foundation.*

They came about through governmental collaboration and agreements, and not as a result of the will and the work of the peoples who have set these governments in place. They have not grown from the base layer of society, but from its top range.

That is why I am convinced that the Web will be the foundation for the *true union of peoples* in not too distant a future. The Web grew without any governmental control, although it was, paradoxically, created for governmental purposes. Yet from the moment it was given to the public by the military agencies that had created it, it was a free landscape for new discoveries. And it quickly grew beyond national borders and cultures.

My idea may seem uncanny. Consider that also on the national level, stability was reached only from the moment that the peoples themselves chose their governments.

This is not so much a function of the constitutional system which can be monarchical or republican. As long as a king or ruler is firmly based upon the trust of his people, his government will bring about effective solutions and bear fruits. Some of the old Chinese kings who based their rulership upon the true interest of their people and universal laws have given abundant evidence to this historical and political fact. On the other hand, the best republican government that is corrupt and has lost the trust of a majority of citizens will disappear sooner or later and leave a vacuum of frustration and a bad taste in the mouth of the populace.

What only counts is that the system is truly democratic, which means not democratic on paper. On both the national and the international level, democracy brings about stability. Governments who do not enjoy the backup of their peoples reign in *unstable conditions* and can be thrown over by social unrest and upheaval.

Present international organizations are for the great majority established 'from above,' without the necessary democratic elections from the side of the peoples, in a process that is not transparent to the citizen. This is one of the reasons why the 'man in the street,' be it in the West or the East, when asked about the United Nations or similar organizations, either admits ignorance and gives a negative or indifferent judgment. This is simply so, and understandable because they have not been directly involved in the creation of the organization or the election of its staff.

How can these organizations then seriously attempt to build a future world government? They would reign over people who do not even know them. Therefore, if these organizations, as it seems now, are unable to allow reforms, they will disappear.

This is in part also valid for the European Union. That is why a few years ago the European Parliament was fundamentally reformed and direct elections for the European parliamentarians have been institutionalized. In the public opinion all over Europe this step was considered as a progress of the unification progress, although skepticism prevailed as to how the European Union will practically carry out the will of the peoples at its basis, and not only the will of their governments or top-class industrials.

The Web has grown from the root up, and not from the branches down, as all our present political international organizations did. Therefore, the chance that my prediction will come true is, I think, higher than the chance that it will not. For it is much easier and much more effective to learn a healthy body perform more functions than to teach a sick and dysfunctional body to perform even very few basic functions.

And the present international organizations are not only sick and dysfunctional, they waste human and financial resources to an extent that their maintenance equals ruin for all those who, willingly or unwillingly, have to finance them. And that is all of us.

The Value of Vision

Just as the book, after the invention of the printing press, revolutionized the world and our lifestyle, the e-book gave us another revolution.

Not only because the e-book is read onscreen, but because this kind of book is a multimedia book. The fantasy of the reader will not be left on its own, as before, but actively stimulated by multimedia links such as photos, videos and interactive functions. For anybody who today doubts the success of the e-book, while Adobe® Corporation initially was at pains with turning their huge investments in the e-book market profitable, now it's notorious that, for example, Amazon® Kindle® is a resounding success. This market continues to grow, and the amazing thing is that the book market grows simultaneously, while still some years ago, predictions were dim as to the book being able to compete with the e-book.

The obvious advantage of the electronic book is that it can combine authoring with embedding virtual reality to create the photorealistic picture of an artistically created world. Visions are reality in the imaginary realm. Not only that they create virtual reality and are necessary predecessors of any creation, vision is by itself a form of reality. A vision is not a tool only, it is a form of being, not a seed only, but a fully grown tree.

Visions form an invisible reality behind the visible one. They directly tap into what Plato called *eidos* (ideas).

You could imagine this world of vision which is universal, as a second reality, another virtual reality that is hidden for our senses yet real for our mind, our nonsensory perception and our imagination.

The visualization of new reality is not only a creative game, but creation in itself. This is a subtle difference. Many people grasp that imagination has creative power, yet only a few will admit that imagination represents a world in itself, another reality which is already existent, or existential, and not only a potentiality for the creation of future existential reality.

Human creation is basically built upon visions. Visions are at the origin of all human progress. The word vision originally means 'sight.' We *see* into the future, or into a better reality, with our inner eye. And we *foresee* events or things before the time is ripe for them or the technological standard is existent to produce them in tangible reality.

Our inner visions are situated outside the time-space continuum. They are part of universal intelligence which precedes the time-bound and earth-bound continuum and which is eternal.

Our children grow into the information age without hurt; many, before they touch the keyboard of a PC, know to manage their game boys and video games. Since the logic and often also the handling of electronic devices are similar, our children often are our masters and teachers, and more, our consultants in all what concerns the essential bones of the global information network.

Common sense and practical reasons speak for a much stronger implication of the next generation into the actual growth process of the Internet. If our governments do not care about a *transformation of the educational systems,* private institutions will and a growing number of parents shall send their children to alternative schooling.

Children sitting through their most learn-intensive age on 19th century school benches with no access to technology are educated towards being either slaves or cultural cripples in the near future. Those children will have to learn later on, with more effort and perhaps less pleasure what they could have learned by playing in their early age. We are confronted with the fact daily. People loose their jobs because of the restructuring of the global industrial network, the different use and availability of resources, changing technologies and lifestyles, and a rapidly growing turn from a nation-centered economy to an international one.

This makes for a large number of people worldwide who are in transition from job to job, and from place to place. Some never understand that in our times, we have to learn constantly. Those remain jobless.

Others learn to learn and to re-learn; they are flexible or have learned to be flexible. They will find new, and perhaps more fulfilling jobs or realization opportunities.

Some of them become outstanding examples of entrepreneurship, simply because they took a passion for one or the other of the new technologies and put all their energy in a project that changed not only their life, but also their social standard.

But for all of us, the new values impact upon our career choices and the way we live our professional lives. While in the past, one usually had one career covering one's entire professional life cycle, this process, as the new values take hold, becomes more short-lived and people are thus forced to be as versatile as possible for keeping afloat in the global job market.

Points to Ponder

▸ *Chapter Six* was about the *new values*, the values that are valid for the information age, New Age or Aquarius Age. It has to be seen that we are currently undergoing a millenary transformation if not revolution in both social and natural sciences, in psychology, medicine and healing, as well as in matters of religious belonging and spirituality.

▸ The change of values is so fundamental that it grabs at all paradigms at once, not just at our science paradigm; no paradigm shall remain untouched from this fundamental change. The nature of the transition from the *Pisces Age* to the *Aquarius Age*, we are currently undergoing globally is so drastic that all paradigms will change accordingly, in their integrality, not one by one.

▸ However, as Fritjof Capra showed clearly in *The Tao of Physics (1975/1984/2000)* and *The Turning Point (1982/1987)*, there are certain paradigms, such as the science paradigm, that are leading the pace, at least at the beginning of the transformation process.

▸ The first fundamental value, which was unheard of in the *Pisces Age* yet is basic to the *Aquarius Age* is the *Value of Systemic Thinking*. It is for this reason that systems research, a branch of science created during the 20th century, is around today, and was not before, while the idea is well part of perennial science. (In this sense, the old Hermetic science was truly systemic, as Manly P. Hall affirms in *The Secret Teachings of All Ages (1928/2003).*

▸ The second fundamental value for the *Aquarius Age* is the *Value of Individuality*, while under the *Pisces Age*, the group was valued higher than the person in the group. Accordingly, the trend currently is away from herd thinking and toward individualized expression; this is why *originality*, not imitation, is what will be rewarded in the future. This also means that the societal tolerance level for individual opinions and lifestyles is on the rise.

▸ Next, the value of *Social Diversity* is characteristic for the *Aquarius Age*, which is really the opposite of the social and religious uniformity that was the social ideal under the *Pisces Age*.

239

- Another value to be emphasized for the decades and centuries to come is *Permissiveness*, especially in the form of *permissive education*.

- A value that can be felt already now is the *Value of Boundless Self-Expression*. Computers, the Internet, the new self-publishing opportunities for text and media, all this expands the range of self-expression for the modern citizen beyond what has ever existed previously in human history. And most importantly, within self-publishing, a realm of personal freedom has been achieved, that was not achieved in online publishing. I am speaking about publishing that is not censored.

- In a networked international business culture, the importance of the value of *Global Cooperation* will be increasing with each year.

- The same is true for the value of *Self-Regulation*, inherent in the functioning of all living systems. More the culture gets back on the side of love and away from the side of moralism, the more it will be grounded in self-regulatory control, which is natural and non-coercive, contrary to the coercive brutal persecutory social and legal control systems built in Pisces culture.

- Finally, the values of *Political Transparence* and *Vision* will not only be important, but crucial for the very survival of the human race and its growth beyond the boundaries of the *Pisces Age*.

Chapter Seven

Handle Power

Positive Self-Empowerment

In this sub-chapter we work on our inner power, self-esteem, potential, our soul values and the necessary trust-building with life and ourselves.

In *Positive Self-Empowerment (PSE)* we are learning and applying a technique that helps us build our inner powers and at the same time develop relationships that are harmonious and mutually beneficial.

In *Positive Self-Talk (PST)*, the next sub-chapter, we are looking at acting behind the mask, focusing inside and finding more constructive ways of dealing with our daily self-talk.

My approach to self-empowerment can be shown in three easy steps you should work through for repeating the principles and relating powerfully yet respectfully to others.

Step 1

Acknowledge Your Power Needs

Step 2

Stop Disempowering Others

Step 3

Make the New Pattern Work

Step 1 - Acknowledge Your Power

Positive Self-Empowerment (PSE) is a simple tool to work for reaching these three goals step by step. There must always be a first step, and sometimes it's the most difficult one. The first step in PSE is recognizing your *need for power*. The question why we need power may seem provocative, and at the same time simplistic.

Power often is associated only with its negative aspect, as a way to dominate others or taking advantage of others.

The reason is that most people do not know how to handle their natural self-power or primary power in a true and rightful way, that is, in a way not to harm others. What contributes to this confusion is that the mass media display power as good as always as negative, abusive and destructive.

Now let us ask, what actually is primary power? Primary power is a concept I created to connote our original power, and which is distinct from the harmful secondary powers or worldly powers that profoundly mark our current society, and which are clearly violence-inducing, and in the long run damaging the human potential and natural human spirituality.

It must be seen that our international media today are operating largely without an ethical foundation; the foundation of most reporters' business attitude is mere financial success. Stories that are abrasive, accusatory, cynical and negative find acclaim with the general audience, and they simply sell better than well-balanced stories that display life as it really is, a million of shades of gray.

In fact, when we observe what happens when power is absent or denied, we find that it is exactly *disempowerment*, and not power, that drives to abuse, and that it is the absence of power that leads to chaotic behavior. When we feel strong and powerful, we feel good—and we are good. It is really as simple as that.

Today, the concept of so-called 'personal power' has become fashionable in the training world, in management, in business. It is widely recognized that we need personal power not only as leaders but in our quality as simple human beings who want to be respected for what we are and at the same time relate to others in a way to share positive powerful feelings and experiences. As we have learnt already, what happens in such exchanges, when there is a balance of powers, is that people build *true synergy*.

Synergistic relationships are characterized by the fact that everybody involved feels powerful and that there are no power struggles. Synergy is probably an abbreviation of the term 'synergetic energy' which means something like combined or fusioned energy. *Merriam-Webster's Dictionary* defines:

> **syn•er•gism** n : interaction of discrete agencies (as industrial firms), agents (as drugs), or conditions such that the total effect is greater than the sum of the individual effects — syn•er•gist n — syn•er•gis•tic adj — syn•er•gis•ti•cal•ly adv
>
> © 1994 by Merriam-Webster, Incorporated.

The condition for synergy is that we individually recognize our *need for power* and, based on this insight, honor the other's need for power. The reason why many people refuse power is that they refuse *responsibility*. They refuse to lead their own destiny. They refuse to reign over their own kingdom.

So my simple suggestion is that *you give yourself your power back!* Even if we work together on it, it's you who will give you more power, not me. I can't empower you if you don't participate in the process. I can only show you some ways how you can avoid to constantly disempower yourself and how you can gain your power back, as I went through the same process, down and up again, and therefore I may be able to share it with you.

Otherwise I couldn't. *I am not teaching something.* In my view, there is nothing to teach in self-empowerment and personal growth training, because there is nothing to learn. I'm not a seminar teacher, and you are not my student. I refuse to be a guru even if others want to put me into this role. It wouldn't be honest from my part. That is why I am talking of sharing experience with you. That's all I can do.

Step 2 - Stop Disempowering Others

The second step in PSE is to *empower yourself instead of disempowering others.* The problem most of us have is that we consciously or unconsciously feed on the power of others. It means that we at times absorb their vital energy in order to have more energy ourselves. For most people this is unfortunately an entirely unconscious process. However, once we gain awareness of our *own power pattern,* we tend to have greater awareness of the power of others. For example, instead of making somebody down by feeding on this person's vital energy, I can look to tender my own garden first. If the mistake was really with the other, I can take a chance to empower that person to a point that he or she will *assume responsibility* and thus do something about the mistake. And at the same time I can use the opportunity to signal that person that I am *supportive and caring.*

The result will be that our relationship will *greatly improve.* There will be more synergy between us, more understanding and more openness. There will be more trust.

Self-empowerment in my understanding creates positive reality in transforming our thought structures. In fact, many of us are driven by a negative inner program which was usually built in early childhood. These programs drive us unconsciously and if they are negative, they bring about frustration and unsatisfying life experiences. This is because inner programs are composed of thought patterns and emotional patterns that, as they are repetitive, hold us within a vicious circle of frustrating life experiences which in turn seem to justify or confirm our negative worldview.

Positive reality and success, happiness and fulfillment are no chance; they are programmed! However, the will and intention alone to change your inner program or script are not enough. This is so because much of our inner program is unconscious. It means that we are not aware of it and have the impression that all comes from outside to us. Therefore, the first thing to do for implementing change is to accept that we are *not driven by outside forces, nor other human beings,* but uniquely by ourselves. When I see that I program my destiny, and not others or society, I will perhaps want to sincerely apologize for having projected my inner failures onto others; then I might want to admit that I am the only creator and designer of my destiny. It really means that we have to forgive others and ourselves, and this regularly, just like something we do naturally, like an attitude.

Ostrander & Schroeder write in *Superlearning 2000* that for them personally to get on in their lives, forgiving others was essential. If we want revenge we take it first on ourselves, wherefore these authors came to be convinced that *living well is the best revenge*. With this conscious attitude we are open to access our inner program if we use relaxation or meditation or some form of spontaneous art in order to get more connected to our subconscious mind. In the relaxed state then, we give to ourselves positive suggestions which deeply penetrate into our subconscious mind, and so much the more when we repeat this procedure several times a day over a certain period of time.

Step 3 - Make the New Pattern Work

The third step in PSE is to make your new script work. How to implement new life scripts, how to change our inner programs, how to positively influence our attitude?

Our two brain hemispheres carry out different tasks and are organized in a different way, and brain waves of different length and amplitude induce a different psychosomatic condition or state of mind:

Delta waves (0.5 – 4 Hz)

Delta is the frequency range up to 4 Hz. It tends to be the highest in amplitude and the slowest waves. It is seen normally in adults in slow wave sleep. It is also seen normally in babies. It is usually most prominent frontally in adults.

Theta waves (4 – 7 Hz)

Theta is the frequency range from 4 Hz to 7 Hz. Theta is seen normally in young children. It may be seen in drowsiness or arousal in older children and adults; it can also be seen in meditation. This range has been associated with reports of relaxed, meditative, and creative states.

Alpha waves (8 – 14 Hz)

Alpha is the frequency range from 8 Hz to 14 Hz. Hans Berger named the first rhythmic EEG activity he saw, the *alpha wave*. It is brought out by closing the eyes and by relaxation. It was noted to attenuate with eye opening or mental exertion.

Beta waves (14 – 30 Hz)

Beta is the frequency range from 14 Hz to about 30 Hz. It is seen usually on both sides in symmetrical distribution and is most evident frontally. Low amplitude beta with multiple and varying frequencies is often associated with active, busy or anxious thinking and active concentration. It is the dominant rhythm in patients who are alert or anxious or who have their eyes open.

Gamma waves (30 – 100 Hz)

Gamma is the frequency range approximately 26 to 100 Hz. Gamma rhythms are thought to represent binding of different populations of neurons together into a network for the purpose of carrying out a certain cognitive or motor function.

We reach our full creative potential only when we involve both our brain hemispheres equally in our thought processes. This means that thinking needs to be coordinated in such a way that we profit from the specialties of each brain hemisphere by combining them into one *whole integrated thought process* that is based on the harmonious functioning of the *full brain*.

Not only learning speed and ability but our entire creative potential is greatly enhanced from the moment we use the full brain and not only one brain hemisphere. With our brain hemispheres it's a bit like with the potentialities of two persons. We cannot say that one plus one equals two when we talk of two people brainstorming for new solutions. We all know that in this case we have a multiplication factor built in the cooperation of these two people.

That is why we can say that in terms of human potential, one plus one can result in millions. The same potentiality is true for results achieved by coordinating our brain hemispheres.

Now, how can self-empowerment positively affect our personal reality? Let me explain it step by step.

Relaxation puts our brain into the so-called *alpha-state*, a state of higher receptivity, which equally brings about a higher coordination of our two brain hemispheres. Let me tell you a bit more about the method itself, how I practiced it, for example, in a train-the-trainers program for an elite unit of the Indonesian government, in 1998. First, the participants receive a rather astute mental preparation for the experience. Why? It's important to know what's going to happen. To experience a state of hypnotic trance for about half an hour is generally not a day-to-day experience for government officials, nor for most other people. For avoiding from the start any stress-related reactions resulting from resistance, there is only one way, information and again information in the form of mental preparation. This is the basic setup:

- You stretch out comfortably;

- You listen with headphones to specially composed music;

- You go through seven phases into deep relaxation;

- You get acquainted with positive suggestions or prayers;

- You learn to give positive suggestions to yourself;

- You learn ways to change your inner script.

Relaxation that is effected through music is especially deep as music has the special advantage to impact easily on brain coordination and positively affects our vibrational body, the luminous energy field. But it can be done with physical exercises as well, if preferred.

In my experience, positive self-empowerment works without effort which makes it so powerful and attractive. Not that most people are lazy; the reason is that in general what enhances the mental setup is succeeding more easily when it is devoid of effort.

Learning by playing and the amazing learning successes it books, for example in Japan, is largely confirming this observation. Learning is more efficient, more effective when it is pleasurable and effortless. This brought me to the conclusion that *our brain dislikes effort and likes comfort,* which is an insight that shows why the traditional school system must fail and ever failed!

Studying the lives of geniuses shows very clearly that they dislike hard and ineffective learning, which is why many of them drop out of school; yet they learn x times easier and faster than the average dummy. Why? Because they develop individual learning techniques which combine learning and pleasure so that they can derive pleasure from learning.

To do this, the first thing is having a *motivation for learning*. It means that the stuff we want to learn must *interest* us. Nobody can derive pleasure from learning something that they consider irrelevant or uninteresting, or really off-track. So the first step in effective learning is finding out what is our field of interest, where is our talent.

When we practice PSE we receive, directly or after a while, flashes of insight or we take spontaneous initiatives which show us what we are really interested in. It often happens that participants say that they knew it already since a long time that they want to do something about it, yet did not think it was 'that important.'

Intuitively we know everything about ourselves, yet often we do not regard intuitions as a *serious source of insight and knowledge*. Our culture and educational system do not favor this source of knowledge and even destroy it more or less.

One powerful positive suggestion regarding our learning motivation and ability is for example:

Learning is always easy and enjoyable for me.

For teachers (who are also learning-teachers, persons who should be able to train learning motivation and skills), the corresponding formula would be:

Teaching is always easy and enjoyable for me.

The enthusiastic teacher, the one who teaches with joy because he or she derives pleasure from teaching, transmits automatically the message that the learning process is a joyful and pleasurable one, even without verbally teaching learning skills. What are learning skills for?

No learning skill can transmit to the student the *pleasure* learning can provide, no learning technique can build the inner motivation for learning. A technique is a technique, nothing more and nothing less; it's simply a tool.

Yet techniques do not generally affect our inner attitudes, our motivation, our mental attitude. I do not talk now about mind-techniques, of course. When I talk about techniques, I am talking about what you are used to call *skills*. I talk about techniques like a piano technique, a typewriting technique, a management technique, a car-driving technique or a mathematical technique, and so on.

We should rather avoid extremes and not put stress on the body. If we appeal to our inner wisdom and develop confidence that this wisdom always guides us in the right speed, we will progress sound and safe, and not to the detriment of some part of us, be it body or mind. Especially people who want to achieve high, who have high goals, who think big, are inclined to sacrifice at times some of their resources, because they think this sacrifice helps them to surpass themselves and to go beyond their limits. Afterwards they may however find out that nothing can be achieved on a long-term basis *if we pursue it from outside of our center,* based upon mere willpower, and not from within our total being.

There are basic suggestions that open our inner potential. Once we are in deep relaxation and our mind is relaxed and receptive, we affirm:

Every day, in all areas of my life, I feel better and better.

This simple suggestion, developed by Dr. Émile Coué in France, effects miracles. Dr. Coué was one of the first pioneers of suggestive healing. In his hospital in Nancy, France, he let his patients repeat this powerful mantra while they were in relaxation or doing some repetitive activity such as sewing, weaving or embroidery. This basic mantra can be varied, for example for self-acceptance:

Every day, in all areas of my life, I approve more of myself.

In fact, many people have a problem of *self-acceptance.* What happens when we constantly put others higher than ourselves because we do not really approve of ourselves? We continuously try to *conform to what others expect from us* or rather what we believe they expect from us. As a result, we are out of our center and cannot realize our full potential. In addition, we feel worn out and unhappy. The stress to comply with other people's needs can affect your health and even cause heart disease. A suggestion to counteract this, would be:

Every day more, I realize my full potential from my own center.

When I got acquainted with positive thought, years ago, reading Joseph Murphy's *The Power of Your Subconscious Mind (1963/2000)*, I was especially moved by Dr. Murphy's stressing the necessity to formulate our needs in a way to bring good for all beings, yet to realize them in the first place for ourselves.

After reading Murphy that I was reflecting on my general mental attitude. I found that, strangely enough, I had a nasty habit to constantly sacrifice myself for the benefit of others while deep down in my heart I was not really in favor of myself, nor I did accept myself as I was. This was my point of departure. In fact, I had encountered situations before that time that everybody except me would consider as very unfortunate or unlucky and friends asked me why I was not more vigilant with certain people? Some of my friends said that I let other people walk over my feet and did nothing to defend my position in relationships and socially; in addition, they voiced that I was fatalistic and too passive.

Then I started with Dr. Murphy's scientific prayer system and a few months later I heard from a growing number of people, including my psychiatrist that I had 'completely changed.' I myself was not much aware of it, besides the simple fact that I felt better in my skin, without criticizing myself all the time, without feeling guilty for this and that all the time, and so on. Well-meaning friends also revealed me that before this fundamental change, I had always tried to justify myself to a point to apologize for my very existence.

The concept of *soul power* was at this time still unknown to me. When I entered psychotherapy, I heard from the psychiatrist that I had a problem with my ego structure and lacked intrinsic self-power since I habitually thought of power as something dangerous, negative and abusive.

My psychiatrist, an expert in Erickson hypnotherapy, empowered me in a subtle way, using light hypnosis and a very special form of dialogue which made me aware of all the points I had to work on. I began with the *inner dialogue* as a technique to get in touch with my *inner selves*, a work that I did on my own, but that was actively encouraged by my psychiatrist.

Also did he fully approve of Murphy's prayer therapy which I carried out simultaneously to the work we did together. It appeared that this form of self-empowerment actually coincided well with the therapy, to an extent which amazed and surprised my psychiatrist. He said he had never seen somebody changing so quickly, and so entirely.

During the two years of my psychotherapy I read many publications about *creative visualization* and its use in various therapeutic settings. I studied *sophrology* and saw that it makes active use of creative visualization to achieve peak performance for sport champions all over the world. Thus I got the idea to integrate visualizations into the self-empowerment system I had developed and continued to practice for my benefit. I noted that the practice of positive thought is indeed greatly enhanced by using fantasy images that describe the new reality visually. It is very powerful to imagine that what we want to get is already ours.

However, note that not everybody is good in visualization. Many of us must learn it, and part of the training is of course supporting participants with practical advice and help to build up step by step their inner view, their imagination. Actually, the first step in practicing positive thinking could be drafting a *wish list*, a paper which simply lists what we desire to have or achieve, and then visualizing every item of the list, like in a film, as if it was already fully realized in our life.

Positive Self-Empowerment as a result of my own personal transformation became a tool for success techniques and the foundation of the human skill training I developed later on. From the feedback I got on my work, and as a fruit of many encounters with general managers, human resource directors and executives in different countries of the Asia-Pacific region, I developed a feeling for the importance of offering a training which *actively enhances self-confidence, trust, teambuilding capacities and creative intelligence,* as well as the willingness to assume responsibility.

Self-confidence is the basis of true optimism. It is faith in ourselves, our singularity. In the word self-confidence is contained *self* and *confidence*: confidence in the *self*. The self or higher self, Ramana Maharshi teaches, is our higher instance, or guide, the I-AM force in us. Fairy tales, myths and religions tell us that we should exclusively rely upon the guidance that we receive from this higher direction that we use to call the god-force, the indwelling spirit, or otherwise. If we put it into spiritual terms or simply evaluate it under a scientific perspective, it remains the same truth.

Without believing in ourselves and accepting ourselves at the beginning of work on our potential, we can't achieve anything. Many programs for self-development overlook or belittle the importance of these two basic elements, which makes that these programs do not really go to the root of the problem and that their effectiveness remains limited.

Positive Self-Empowerment goes beyond those limitations and affects the person and the *mask of the personality* as a whole.

It entirely changes our inner program, our mindset and our general attitude toward life, ourselves and others.

Positive Self-Talk

Many people want to get into self-healing today and are searching for some tools to change inner scripts. We've got the tools, quite a bit of them, but we've to *apply* them to get them working in our lives.

What is it that keeps many people away from practicing NLP or any other sophisticated method to change their inner scripting? I guess it is that many of these methods are complex and need to be thoroughly learned and understood before they can be applied. This means sitting down and reading, perhaps five hundred pages of a manual before actually putting it to practice.

And of course, there's always a bit of the author's own making, character and individuality that went into it.

In one word, there's a time problem. And it seems that most people who at all would want to spend time on self-improvement are not the kind to sit around at home doing nothing, but rather busy people who have many priorities on their schedule. Hence the need for a method that is not intellectual but *practical* and that can be flexibly adapted to everybody's needs and preferences is so high.

This guide shows you in small steps that each won't take more than about fifteen minutes of your precious time how to develop—

▸ A positive inner script;

▸ A genuinely positive and creative self-talk;

▸ A personality that is flexible, strong and confident;

▸ A smart way of dealing with emotional conflicts or stress;

Step 1

Positive Self-Talk (PST) is a simple tool to achieve all those goals step by step. There must always be a first step, and sometimes it's the most difficult one. The first step in PST to learn to listen to yourself.

We all engage in self-talk. Actually self-talk is something natural and healthy. Our personalities are composed of different entities or energies. The more creative and original we are, the more clearly distinguished facets are showing up in our character and mindset. We are not just one person. The word 'person' in fact comes from the old Greek *persona* which means *mask*. Our personalities are the masks we wear to adopt different roles and carry them through in life. Nobody seems to have only one role in life. We are naturally multiple actors on multiple stages, playing the partner, the child, the parent, the adult or the employer/employee and other roles at every moment.

As long as we are engaged in a role, we can't listen to the whole of our being, to the person behind the masks. We may be able to listen to the actor, the person, the shell but not to the director, the nucleus, the flame or creative inner self. This creative inner self is our true and undivided being. PST helps us to reach it. You can practice the first step by—

—listening to the *actor*, or by

—listening to the *director.*

I give you complete freedom as to what you find more appropriate to begin with. There are people who want to know right on the spot and sit down, leave their shells and get centered. I would call them the *inside-outs.*

There are others who prefer to begin on the shell level and work from there down inside. These are *outside-ins*.

Only *you* can know to which group you belong!

It can be said that the second group, the outside-ins, are more left-brain oriented whereas the first group, the inside-outs, are more right-brain oriented. How to determine what kind of person you are? There are certain signs or indications in our way of being, our behavior and our usual way of thinking about life and the world that are hints on this matter.

The outside-ins

- are rather gregarious

- tend to act before they think

- tackle problems rather rationally and deductively

- tend to be bold or overreact in stress situations

- imitate if lacking new ideas

The inside-outs

- are rather solitary

- tend to think before they act

- tackle problems rather intuitively and inductively

- tend to hide or make depression in stress situations

> create if lacking new ideas

These two groups are of course just schemes and since life is not to be grasped with schemes, this is only indicative and not definite. We tend to have characteristics actually of both groups. However, most people show in their overall behavior or lifestyle a slight or pronounced tendency for the characteristics of one of the two groups.

Step 2

The second step in PST is to get motivated to change the basic inner script. This can be done with working just five minutes every day on changing the pattern.

Why is it important that we first *set our motivation* before we begin with influencing and changing our self talk? This step is often overlooked.

Most approaches that offer quick fixes are so much involved with the method that they forget the motives behind it. However, effective learning is impossible without having clarity about our motives for the learning experience. Learning is above all a function of the *motivation to learn*. If this basic motivation is lacking, the best method, however ingenious, will not make us masters of the stuff to be learned.

Let me give a simple example. How many of us know a family where a child or even all the children are forced to play a musical instrument like the piano or the cello? And how many of us know that the motivation these children have for learning musical instruments are non-existent. In fact, the true motive for the children to learn to play music is the parents' wish to have musical children.

Sometimes, children are musically gifted and develop by themselves a motivation to learn a musical instrument. However, in those cases the child will usually take the initiative to get lessons or at least an instrument, and not the parent.

Naturally, the motivation to learn must come from the learner! It is an inner expression, something very deep and of course related to our soul, our character or even, if you want, our virtue or karma. This means that if it is forced upon, it's useless, because in terms of character building there is no outside-in. Character building must begin inside and work towards the outside and *not vice versa*.

What those good-meaning parents want in fact is to help building their children's character. However, they apply outside-in methods and therefore they will create obstinacy rather than virtue in their children.

How can you motivate yourself? There are three points to observe:

▸ Take an ultimate decision to change your self-image

▸ Write down on a list all reasons that motivate you for change

▸ Work out a schedule for putting this decision into practice

Example of an Ultimate Decision

> I hereby decide ultimately that I am going to change my inner script, my basic attitude and the reflection of this inner attitude in the outside world. I know that my self-image is made up over the years with all kinds of experiences. I am fully aware of this fact and I know that my life is not dependent on outside circumstances but solely on my own state of mind, my belief system and my overall perception of life. Keeping all this in mind, I hereby take the firm will and intention to build a mindset that fully supports the realization of my personal power and original talents through worthwhile contributions to the whole of humanity and the universe. This mindset also strongly enhances my prosperity, and this in a way that others equally benefit from my inner and outer riches.

Before you sit down to write your list, try to *connect to your inner self,* distance yourself from the outside world for a moment, perhaps looking for a quiet spot in your house or wherever you are and get centered by doing a few deep breaths. Just sit back, close your eyes and breathe deeply and naturally, and feel that your energy centers peacefully in your heart.

You will experience that with this simple method your body tension suddenly releases and you may feel tired, heavy and calm.

There is usually a feeling of hot energy flowing into the heart. You may perceive this right on or later, even some time after the relaxation. Just enjoy this quiet state of mind without searching for something. If thought comes let it pass, if emotions come up let them flow through you naturally. Don't interfere in them. An idea may flush up during the relaxation or later on. Don't let it pass unnoticed, but immediately catch pen and paper and write it down, even if it's vague or seems trivial. Often we judge as trivial inner perceptions simply because we have not fully developed our sixth sense and our rational mind tends to make down those intuitions which are extremely helpful and valuable. Give yourself five minutes of your precious time for this centering exercise each and every day. This alone can cause miracles of positive change!

My Reasons for Change

Instead of making a living I want to lead a prosperous life in which material riches are the natural outflow of my inherent talents and strengths.

Instead of hiding myself behind invisible screens I want to act in public in order to contribute in a positive way to projects and endeavors that enhance life quality, beauty, love and peace on earth.

Instead of aspiring to small or mid-sized goals, I now aspire to the highest goals and ideas I can think of. I know that I can only achieve what I have envisioned. Therefore my vision is now broad and I feel enthusiastic about the perspective that I from now on attract lots of riches, beauty, positive values, love and power into my life.

All what I achieve and all what I stand for is in accordance with universal laws and destined to contribute to the common good of all living.

Step 3

The third step in PST is to *take action* to implement new positive self-talk. Once you have developed awareness of your self-talk and you see that it is somehow negative and thus detrimental to your growth and natural desire for high achievement, you are in a very favorable position.

Why? You may say that it's not enough to sit back and wait when you have discovered a basic bug in your way to think about life. You may want to do something about it, and massively. However, believe it or not, the very fact that you've become aware of it makes that things change by themselves. It's your subconscious mind that greatly helps you to make the necessary changes.

Why then, you may rightly ask, does this inner mind not act before my getting aware of the problem? The answer is that it does. However, as long as you refuse to build positive awareness, your mind's action frame is very limited. It will constantly try to lead you to that awareness, through circumstances, through books that you suddenly discover, through people you meet, through new activities you discover that did not seem of interest to you before ...

The breakthrough is possible by combining your subconscious and your conscious mind acting in sync. It's this basic synergy that is so powerful and helps you to overcome the most obstinate of limitations.

There are basically *four important rules* for positively changing your self-talk. The first rule is a negative, a don't, the other three are positive or do's:

—Rule One: Don't interfere in your self-talk, don't judge, don't punish

—Rule Two: Put behind every negative thought a positive thought

—Rule Three: Build a positive-thought pool

—Rule Four: Build Focus

Rule One

Watch what's going on inside the box

It's very important that from the start you develop a correct attitude in dealing with yourself. You can't expect yourself becoming a leader as long as you treat yourself like a slave!

If you want to get royalties out of your life, treat yourself royally! This means that you do not fight against yourself nor punish yourself nor build in your life a system of *'punishment and reward.'*

This latter system may be good for training dogs but it's against human dignity. It namely will eventually tear down your self-esteem. I know that many quick-fix kind of approaches to self-improvement use similar techniques.

They may get quick results but those results vanish off after some time, or are even counterproductive. This is so because they build within you even more blind spots than you had before you engaged in such kind of activity. In all matters of human evolution and in building attitude, quick fixes simply won't work!

What happens if you don't respect the first rule? You will create war within yourself inner conflict that is going to block you from experiencing peace of mind. And without basic peace of mind, no change in character, habits or attitude can be expected. Peace of mind is the preliminary condition for any kind of evolution you want to make.

This is why religious scriptures, from whatever religion are so seriously emphasizing the importance of creating peace in us and around us. Peace of mind is essential for getting connected to our deep-down reservoir of wisdom and energy and the guidance we receive from the invisible world. The more we experience peace, the more our life will gain significance and our circle of influence broaden.

Respecting yourself means to *accept yourself* in the first place! It also means to passively acknowledge the status quo of your life, not out of a quietist or even fatalist position, but as a *simple starting point*. If you refuse to acknowledge the present, with all what it implies, you can't move into the future. You'll be stuck in the past. We all have the choice to move forward or backward on the scale of time.

Nobody forces you to choose evolution if you decide for regression.

However, life rather tends to favor evolution. It's in the way the energy moves. Therefore it's actually much easier to live on ways that favor evolution than to retrograde back in the past or to be stuck to a stagnant present.

Nowadays, we live in a strong field of regression, especially in the countries that are the most advanced in evolution. That's part of life's paradoxical nature. Where there is much light, there is much shadow. We can choose to walk in light or in darkness. Recognizing that there is both light in shadow and shadow in light, as there is *yang* in *yin* and *yin* in *yang*, we can make a conscious decision as to the main paradigms we accept to be valid for our lives.

Behold, your negative self-talk is not something to be fired away, dismissed or silenced. Life is not maintained and enhanced by killing. And virtue not by killing vice. As long as we think that we have to eradicate 'bad weeds' in order to breed good ones, we act counter to the very principles of life. A bad weed is 'bad' only in the sense that it grows in the wrong place. Moss that grows among roses is considered a bad weed. But what about a rose growing in an acre of potatoes?

It's very relative what is bad and good; it all depends. Life, nature does not eradicate. It does not produce terminators. Only humans do, and not the most intelligent ones, to be true. The sun shines on all beings. And that's how you should shine on both your positive and your negative self-talk.

What you can do after this first insight is to just passively watch the nature of your self-talk. Then what happens is that your negative self-talk will convey you important messages about yourself, because *there are reasons why you are negative, pessimistic or even bitter about things, events or people.* There are reasons why you are depressed, why your self-talk is making you or others down. To be open to find out, to refrain from judging yourself or others, to be passively watchful what's going on inside of you and, first of all, to be motivated to improve your success abilities, your life quality, your happiness, your service, your standing, how you present yourself to others is essential. As I pointed out already above, your inner motivation alone makes for progress even if you remain passive. However, you can really bring about a major breakthrough, a kind of explosion in success, achievement and long-term opportunities if you do more than just creating the motivation and really get into action.

Rule Two

Act positively upon your self-talk

Action that has been thoroughly prepared from inside-out, and is rooted in a deep inner motivation which is in turn based upon an attitude is extremely powerful!

It's what trainers like Anthony Robbins use to call *massive action!* It's not massive because you jump out of your shell like a Jack-in-the-Box. It's massive because it's deeply rooted in your power potential. What is your power potential? Your power potential is the resource you carry within you, and it's first of all your attitude and the values that this attitude is built upon.

Well then, you may argue, what you offer me here is not a practical method because you want me to change from inside-out and not just change my self-talk. Well, yes, it's not a quick fix, indeed. I don't offer you a cheap kind of *do-this, do-that* approach. That's superficial and will not last. Doing things effectively doesn't mean doing them theoretically, it does not mean we are impractical. Practice that is effective always is founded upon a sound theory. Or have you ever seen a good carpenter who does not know the basic theory of carpentry? Do you know a good computer programmer who does not know how a computer works internally? Often we learn theory by doing and practicing but that does not mean that practice replaces theory. How we learn the theory may be different. It can be caught from books or by doing practical work. But it remains the theory.

The same is valid for self-improvement and the acquisition of leadership skills. In order to improve your self-talk you need some theoretical knowledge about how your mind works. You need to know, for example, that you can't eradicate bad or destructive self-talk just by trying to forget about it or by forcing yourself to not do it. If you work that way you violate yourself and you violate the principles life is based upon; what you then do is to be violent with yourself, simply that!

As I mentioned already, life can't be maintained let alone improved by killing things, by terminating habits and so on. What you create by forcing yourself is only *resistance, blockages, frustration and unhappiness.* And there is more. If you want to force the mind to obey you, the mind will ask you who you are that you can command it? Ask yourself what in you can pretend to be stronger or more powerful than your mind? You may answer: my character, or, my soul. Yes, but your character or your soul do not need to force your mind simply because your mind is not willing to collaborate with them. Why not? Because the mind is composed of past experiences, of memory, of repetitive patterns, habits, survival reactions that have perhaps been useful in the past but are definitely inappropriate in a new and different situation. How then, you may insist, can you get this mind to be more flexible, to be less rooted in the past, to react more appropriately to my present tasks and challenges?

That's really the key question. If you've got there you've got far. The answer is that your mind will act that way if you—

- refrain from disciplining your mind;

- refrain from judging your mind;

> ▸ refrain from punishing your mind;

> ▸ refrain from forcing your mind.

Instead simply acknowledge the state of mind you are in at any given moment! Just find out what your mind is like in a given situation. My mind is confused right now, you may find. My mind is driven by contradictory desires or wishes, you may conclude. So then, stating that fact, what to do further? Not much. Since we agreed that the mind can't be forced and that's no easy way to change old habits that are rooted in our past without getting back into this past (what we really want to avoid because we don't have the time nor the money to follow six years of psycho-therapy), there is only one way of doing. When your mind says A and you know that A is destructive for you, you let your mind say A, but *you* say B. This means if your self-talk is negative you let it be negative. You just put behind the negative sentence that you've trapped a positive one. Example: You trap yourself having had the following inner dialogue:

> A is really a dread. Not only does he cheat me, but he's ugly, mean and stupid. He's done that to others, too. He's a real jerk. And I could kick myself in the ass that I trusted him. I'm not much better in fact. Otherwise I wouldn't have got to make friends with guys like him in the first place. I was always this kind of naive and childish and I would like to really eradicate this idiotic immature behavior in myself. What an ass I was, no!

Now, you don't interfere, you *don't judge,* either. You *do not blame yourself* for this quite negative piece of inner dialogue. Instead, you simply put a positive scene behind it. Something like that:

> A is a godlike being just like me. I affirm that this man is my friend since I followed my inner wisdom to make friends with him. That he acted against universal principles is something serious but as his friend I am called upon to inform him about his mistake. I now take this responsibility serious and get in touch with A to help him affront this mistake and correct it. There will be a way to get in honest dialogue with him. I affirm that my inner child knows that my basic naiveté is part of my innocence and I want to keep this innocence because it's one of the most precious things life has given to me. I've acted right until now and I continue acting right and life will do the rest. A will see his positive qualities from now on and this energy will strengthen those qualities in A and eventually help him transform his weaknesses into strengths.

Rule Three

Build a positive-thought pool

Now you can go a step ahead and not only act occasionally, every time you trap a negative thought pattern, but engage in some kind of prevention! You can build a *positive-thought pool.* That's something similar to a talent pool. What you pool instead are not talents, but thoughts!

A positive-thought pool is an inner reservoir of strength that you can compare to a fountain of light, force and wisdom. It is composed of a variety of positive thought patterns that are ingrained in your mind. Now, what happens if you have built such kind of positive-thought pool? The pattern created is a growth pattern, a pattern in your mind that grows, like a fertile plant that is watered and cared for in the right way. It's our personal success library, a library that is not just dead paper but living content! Two questions arise:

—What are the thoughts that effect growth?

—How can such thought become deeply ingrained in my mind?

The thoughts or thought patterns that effect growth are like seeds. They contain a nucleus which is *bundled mind energy*, an energy that you may imagine of as highly condensed, so condensed that even small quantities of it can bring almost miraculous results.

The reason why these thoughts have intrinsic power simply is the result of their being an outflow of universal principles. What are universal principles? Universal principles, also known as cosmic principles, are rules and laws that are eternal and unchanging, timeless and valid for all beings.

Stephen R. Covey defines principles as 'guidelines for human conduct that are proven to have enduring, permanent value.' You may agree with that but remain skeptical what is going to root those thoughts so deeply in you that they act like an inner script? The secret is simply that they have to be implanted in your subconscious mind. How to get there?

By building focus and doing positive affirmations and by building the strong conviction that your higher destiny will guide you for your best on your way to success. Doing this, you will be clearing your past without ever consciously doing it; it will be done by your consciousness.

Rule Four

Build Focus

Building focus is among the most revealing and rewarding experiences of the self. And yet it's so easy, so utterly simple. You just sit back, close your eyes and visualize a beam of white light that connects your heart with the heart of the universe. You can do this in just five or ten minutes and at any place where you feel safe enough to abandon control.

When you center within yourself you may, perhaps for the first time, become aware of your self-talk. If you have developed already awareness of your self-talk, you can use focusing to recharge you with energy.

However, this is only possible if you can establish silence in your mind. That means you must have worked in some way already on your self-talk. Without that work, self-talk tends to be chaotic in some way, in the sense that it is completely involuntary, like a wild untamed horse.

Behold that focusing gets you much farther than self-talk awareness. Once your mind is sufficiently silent, focusing becomes a powerful experience of connecting yourself with universal wisdom and being recharged by it.

You can then pray silently in your heart and ask for guidance, for light or for more energy to accomplish certain tasks. And don't doubt: it will be given to you!

The Power of Intent

Intent is something like *purposeful and deliberate belief* that is so genuine and strong that there is no doubt left in it. Some of us need to go a long way to really build powerful intention, because to be to that level convinced is a matter of trust. If you deeply mistrust others you will be at odds with the conviction that synergy is one of the strongest forces; as a result, you are at pains formulating the intention to build synergy with others. In other words, if you who have been hurt a lot in life, you naturally are at pains with building that high level of trust with others, and with life. You may not easily understand that synergy with others can only be to your benefit.

If I doubt that nature is basically good and that our human nature is always striving for evolution, I will have a problem with building a conviction of the *existence of a strong positive intention* that guides us always to our best.

Or I try to disintegrate this force from nature and say 'Well, I call it God and it's not part of nature. It has well created nature but itself is outside of it.' Honestly, I doubt that people with such religious concepts can build trust in nature and help nature and the earth to survive. Those beliefs will rather bring about an attitude to disregard nature, if they not endorse rape and dominate nature, or even destroy it. In having disintegrated their God concept from its root, nature, such 'believers' destroy their God's very creation, and most of the time without being aware of their religious perversion.

Intention is so strong that it does not need constant reaffirmation or confirmation. It is like a place in your heart where there is no fear. Fear is perhaps the only thing that can corrupt intent. Fear is destructive anyway. It keeps us from acting appropriately in the ever-changing flow of life. It makes us to keep stuck to old concepts and rigid ideas.

Therefore, in creating positive self-talk as part of a generally positive and creative attitude, we have to cope with our inner or *psychological fear*. We have to find out its origin. And we do this first of all by clearing our past.

Psychological fear has its roots in the past, in past hurt and trauma we went through as children or adolescents or even as young adults. It also may have its origin in former lives, or as a result of karma.

If you disregard the fear-factor, you will remain superficial in your task to create positive self-talk. I do not suggest that you follow a six-year psychotherapy, although I do not say anything against it either. If you listen inside, you will find out what it is that fits you best to clear your past. Here are some of the possible ways:

- Keep a dream journal;

- Work with positive dream visualization;

- Keep a journal or diary;

- Write an autobiography;

- Pray with the firm intention to forgive all people who have hurt you;

- Find out your control drama or survival childhood hangup;

- Get professional help that you feel good with;

- Practice spontaneous art or dance to express your emotions;

- Get to dialogue with your inner selves.

I myself have practiced all of these possible ways, and I can say that all of them work. However, at some times in your life you may have a preference for one or the other. For example, if there is an opportunity to get professional help because at a time you've a friend who is in the business of counseling or therapy or you can afford a therapy anyway or you develop a spontaneous interest for a specific therapeutic approach, you should engage in that way as long as you feel it is good for you. At other times, you may want to pursue your self-healing in a more solitary way. That's fine, too.

If you study the life stories of highly successful people, be it in science, art or business, you will find that most of them went through painful control or survival dramas to get back to their true nature. However, their strength was not to surrender but to continue their way to realize their highest potential, their intrinsic talent, their mission.

Points to Ponder

- In *Chapter Seven* I showed you how to handle your inner powers, boost your potential and fully realize your innate gifts and talents. Of course, to achieve it in your life, you have to *do the work* that leads you there. I can only show you the way, by offering you some techniques that have worked for me, but it's up to you to implement them in your life.

- The methods I presented and explained are *Positive Self-Empowerment (PSE)* and *Positive Self-Talk (PST)*. I have used and applied these techniques in my own personal growth work since about twenty years, and have taught and applied them also in my work with groups in government and industry, to this day. So they have been time-tested and proven their usefulness.

- *Positive Self-Empowerment (PSE)*, is a method the combines the benefits of positive affirmations with creative visualization. The ingredients are not my invention, but well the soup!

- The three basic steps in PSE are to *1) Acknowledge Your Power Needs,* first of all, then *2) Stop to Disempower Others* and *3) Make the New Pattern Work.* In my experience, people who have never done any power work get stuck already at step 1 for the simple reason that they *reject* power, not understanding what it is, and what it is *not,* and then *project* it on others, those they admire, those they venerate, their gurus, saints and power coaches. And yet, without acknowledging your *need for power,* you are getting nowhere. However, be aware that power, or *primary power,* in the sense I am using it, actually means *love*—not any force that dominates others and self.

- Once people have done that first important step, they quite easily see that disempowering others has bad karmic effects and brings about nothing beneficial, except an energy boost at the expense of another person. But the energy boost is temporary and will be followed by guilt or shame, and it will attract exactly the same back, because what we sow, we shall reap. When the pattern has been ingrained for long, it might be difficult to change it, and it's exactly for that reason that I have combined PSE with PST, because without controlling and purifying your self-talk, you won't be able to break the old pattern, and your residual power hangups.

▸ Step 3 is to make the new pattern work, which means to actually *groove your neuronet with that new behavior,* so that it becomes a natural, spontaneous behavior. This can only be done through relaxation, by connecting back with inside, or in other words, by synchronizing your conscious and unconscious thought interfaces. This can be done both individually and, even more joyfully, in the group setting, when everybody relaxes in an arm chair, enjoying beneficial sounds and music, while repeating a short description of the new behavior as an easy-to-memorize affirmation.

▸ Most people find PSE easier and more fun than PST; this is simply so because we are all a little ashamed when we face our shadow, and with many people, their shadow manifests quite virulently in their self-talk.

▸ Charles W. Leadbeater writes in *The Inner Life (1911)* that many people who appear to be 'decent churchgoers' in this life are suffering in the next because what they have done in their thoughts was virtually *murdering people on a daily basis,* and this for years and decades of their lives. As I am explaining it in this chapter, inner peace and a positive growth cycle will be in your reach only if you commit to transforming your self-talk so that it is constantly positive, uplifting and constructive, or, else that there is no self-talk at all.

▸ Inner silence is ultimately the highest achievement, but as it appears that most Westerners are at pains with the very idea or even afraid of it, I do not emphasize it, but put as the ultimate goal the self-talk that is, while it's ongoing, smooth, pro-life and blessing self and others.

▸ Step 1 in PST is to learn to *passively observe* your self-talk. Many people tend to jump to a conclusion when discussing this subject; they simply deny that they had any self-talk, much like many other people deny that they dream. These people are to a point disconnected from their inner life that they seriously believe they had no self-talk. This is a dangerous illusion for when we deny our inner powers, they tend to control us, and without our being aware of it. This means that in such a case, you are driven by forces you ignore, and this can in the extreme case lead to psychopathic behavior and schizophrenia.

▸ Step 2 in PST is to build the motivation necessary to doing the work diligently and persistently enough so that a positive outcome can be achieved. This is an important step for without motivation, I can promise you that you won't make it to change your self-talk. It's not an easy task at all. If it was easy, the world wouldn't be a mess of violence wherever you look, and people could eventually turn their back to the past, to their past wars, failures and trials and the eternal guilt as a result of being so sluggish, so negligent in the face of the need to build inner transparence and purity. It is absolutely essential that you understand that motivation is all in learning anything or changing anything in life. Without motivation, you are powerless, while when you are motivated and committed enough, you can move mountains.

▸ The best way, I found, to build motivation for changing your self-talk is an *Ultimate Decision and Contract with Yourself*, a piece of paper that you date and sign and that you try to honor as you honor any contracts you have with others. You will find it among the Work Sheets at the end of this guide.

▸ Step 3, then, in PST, is the actual work, the action to implement new positive self-talk. The interesting thing is that you do not really need to do something at this point other than to build total awareness of your ongoing self-talk, without trying to defend it or control it in any way. The work is actually done by your consciousness interface.

▸ Most people are shocked when they first build real awareness of their destructive self-talk. There are four simple rules to observe for changing your self-talk, which you can put in the following slogans:

▸ Don't interfere, don't judge, don't punish. Put behind every negative thought a positive thought.

▸ Build a positive thought-pool. Build Focus.

Bibliography

Contextual Bibliography

Argyris, C.
Empowerment: The Emperor's New Clothes
Harvard Business Review, 76(3), 98-105 (1998)

Bass, B.M.
Bass and Stogdill's Handbook of Leadership
Theory, Research, and Managerial Applications
3rd Edition
New York: John Wiley & Sons, 1990

The Future of Leadership in Learning Organizations
The Journal of Leadership Studies, 7(3), 19-40 (2000)

Barron, Frank X., Montuori, et al. (Eds.)
Creators on Creating
Awakening and Cultivating the Imaginative Mind
(New Consciousness Reader)
New York: P. Tarcher / Putnam, 1997

Block, Peter

Stewardship
Choosing Service Over Self-Interest
San Francisco: Berrett-Koehler, 1996

Borg, James

Persuasion
2nd Edition
New York: Pearson Books, 2008

Branden, Nathaniel

How to Raise Your Self-Esteem
New York: Bantam, 1987

Butler-Bowden, Tom

50 Success Classics
Winning Wisdom for Work & Life From 50 Landmark Books
London: Nicholas Brealey Publishing, 2004

Childre, Doc & Cruyer, Bruce

From Chaos to Coherence
The Power to Change Performance
Boulder Creek, CA: Planetary, 2004

Covey, Stephen R.

The 7 Habits of Highly Effective People
Powerful Lessons in Personal Change
New York: Free Press, 2004
15th Anniversary Edition
First Published in 1989

The 8th Habit
From Effectiveness to Greatness
London: Simon & Schuster, 2004

The 3rd Alternative
Solving Life's Most Difficult Problems
London: Simon & Schuster, 2012

Servant Leadership
Use Your Voice to Serve Others
Leadership Excellence, 23(12), 5-6 (2006)

Cusumano, Michael A., Selby, Richard W.

Microsoft Secrets
How the World's Most Powerful Software Company Creates Technology, Shapes Markets and Manages
New York: Free Press, 1998

De Bono, Edward

The Use of Lateral Thinking
New York: Penguin, 1967

The Mechanism of Mind
New York: Penguin, 1969

Serious Creativity
Using the Power of Lateral Thinking to Create New Ideas
London: HarperCollins, 1996

Sur/Petition
London: HarperCollins, 1993

Tactics
London: HarperCollins, 1993
First published in 1985

DiCarlo, Russell E. (Ed.)

Towards A New World View
Conversations at the Leading Edge
Erie, PA: Epic Publishing, 1996

Gibson, J.L., Ivancevich, J.M., Donnelly, J.H. & Konopaske, R.

Organizations: Behavior, Structure and Processes
New York: McGraw-Hill, 2006

Goleman, Daniel

Emotional Intelligence
New York, Bantam Books, 1995

Greenleaf, R.K.

Servant Leadership
A Journey into the Nature of Legitimate Power and Greatness
Mahwah, N.J.: Paulist Press, 1977

The Servant as Leader
in: The Robert K. Greenleaf Reader
Indianapolis, 1991

On Becoming a Servant Leader
San Francisco: Josey-Bass Publishers, 1996
New York: E.P. Dutton, 1976

Hill, Napoleon

The Law of Success
The Master Wealth-Builder's Complete and Original Lesson
Plan for Achieving Your Dreams
New York: Penguin, 2008
First published in 1928

Hofstede, G.

Cultural Constraints in Management Theories
Academy of Management Executive, 7(1), 81-94 (1993)

Houston, Jean

The Possible Human
A Course in Enhancing Your Physical, Mental, and Creative Abilities
New York: Jeremy P. Tarcher/Putnam, 1982

Hunter, J.C.

The World's Most Powerful Leadership Principle
How to Become a Servant Leader
New York: Crown Business, 2004

Joseph, E.E. & Winston, B.E.

A Correlation of Servant Leadership, Leader Trust, and Organizational Trust
Leadership & Organizational Development Journal, 26(1), 6-22

Kiechel, W.

The Leader as Servant
Fortune, 125, 121-122 (1992)

Krause, Donald G.

Sun Tzu
The Art of War for Executives
London: Nicholas Brealey Publishing, 1995

Kolp, A. & Rea, P.

Leading with Integrity
Cincinnati, OH: Atomic Dog Publishing, 2006

Lee, C. & Zemke, R.

The Search for Spirit in the Workplace
Training, 30, 21-28 (1993)

Lloyd, B.

A New Approach to Leadership
Leadership & Organizational Development Journal, 17(7), 29-32 (1996)

Leonard, George, Murphy, Michael

The Live We Are Given
A Long Term Program for Realizing the
Potential of Body, Mind, Heart and Soul
New York: Jeremy P. Tarcher/Putnam, 1984

Liedloff, Jean

Continuum Concept
In Search of Happiness Lost
New York: Perseus Books, 1986
First published in 1977

Locke, John

Some Thoughts Concerning Education
London, 1690
Reprinted in: The Works of John Locke, 1823
Vol. IX., pp. 6-205

Lowen, Alexander

Bioenergetics
New York: Coward, McGoegham 1975

Depression and the Body
The Biological Basis of Faith and Reality
New York: Penguin, 1992

Fear of Life
New York: Bioenergetic Press, 2003

Joy
The Surrender to the Body and to Life
New York: Penguin, 1995

Narcissism: Denial of the True Self
New York: Macmillan, Collier Books, 1983

Pleasure: A Creative Approach to Life
New York: Bioenergetics Press, 2004
First published in 1970

The Language of the Body
Physical Dynamics of Character Structure
New York: Bioenergetics Press, 2006

Manz, C.C.
The Leadership Wisdom of Jesus
Practical Lessons for Today
San Francisco: Berrett-Koehler Publishers, 1998

McCormick, D.W.
Spirituality and Management
Journal of Managerial Psychology, 9(6), 5-8 (1994

Moore, Thomas
Care of the Soul
A Guide for Cultivating Depth and Sacredness in Everyday Life
New York: Harper & Collins, 1994

Murphy, Michael
The Future of the Body
Explorations into the Further Evolution of Human Nature
New York: Jeremy P. Tarcher/Putnam, 1992

Myers, Tony Pearce
The Soul of Creativity
Insights into the Creative Process
Novato, CA: New World Library, 1999

Naparstek, Belleruth
Your Sixth Sense
Unlocking the Power of Your Intuition
London: HarperCollins, 1998

Oster, M.J.

Vision-Driven Leadership
San Bernardino, CA: Here's Life Publishers, 1991

Pearce Myers, Tony (Editor)

The Soul of Creativity
Insights into the Creative Process
Novato: New World Library, 1999

Pollard, C.W.

The Leader Who Serves
Strategy & Leadership, 49-51 (1997)

Russell, R.F.

The Role of Values in Servant Leadership
Leadership & Organizational Development Journal, 22(2), 76-83 (2001)

Russell, R.F. & Stone, A.G.

A Review of Servant Leadership Attributes
Developing a Practical Model
Leadership & Organizational Development Journal, 23/3), 145-157
(2002)

Sanders, J.O.

Spiritual Leadership
Chicago: Moody Press, 1994
San Rafael, CA: Amber Allen Publishing, 1997

Sarkus, D.J.

Servant Leadership in Safety: Advancing the Cause and Practice
Professional Safety, 41, 26-32 (1996)

Sendaya, S. & Sarros, J.C.

Servant Leadership
Its Origin, Development, and Application in Organizations
Journal of Leadership & Organizational Studies, 9(2), 57-64 (2002)

Spears, L.

Reflections on Robert K. Greenleaf and Servant Leadership
Leadership & Organizational Development Journal, 17(7), 33-35 (1996)

Spears, L.C. & Lawrence, M. (Eds.)

Practicing Servant Leadership
Succeeding through Trust, Bravery, and Forgiveness
San Francisco: Jossey Bass, 2004

Stone, A.G., Russell, R.F. & Patterson, K.

Transformational versus Servant Leadership
A Difference in Leader Focus
Leadership & Organizational Development Journal, 25(4), 349-361
(2004)

Walker, J.

A New Call to Stewardship and Servant Leadership
Nonprofit World, 21(4), 25 (2003)

Welch, Jack

Winning
With Suzy Welch
New York: HarperBusiness, 2005

Zyman, Sergio

The End of Marketing as We Know It
New York: HarperCollins, 2000

Personal Notes